Sixty-ninth Street
Suicide

A Memoir of Divorce, Depression
and Defining My *Why*

Sharon
Greenwald

Minneapolis

Minneapolis

Second Edition December 2022
Sixty-ninth Street Suicide: A Memoir of Divorce, Depression and Defining my Why. Copyright © 2020 by Sharon Greenwald.
All rights reserved.

Published by Wisdom Editions, 6800 France Av S, Edina, MN 55435. No parts of this book may be used or reproduced by any means, graphic, electronic, or mechanical, including photocopying, recording, taping or by any information storage retrieval system, without the written permission of the publisher except in the case of brief quotations embodied in critical articles and reviews.

Printed in the United States of America.
10 9 8 7 6 5 4 3 2

ISBN: 978-1-959770-58-9

Cover and book design by Gary Lindberg

Praise for *Sixty-ninth Street Suicide*

This is not an easy topic to talk about with one person let alone write an entire book to share with the world. It was really well done and the author never shied away from the worst parts of her story. For those that are suffering in a depression, know you aren't alone, and for those loved ones, read this book and you might understand them a little more.

Randi-Lee Bowslaugh, Mental Health Author

It takes an immense amount of courage and strength to journey through depression. Thank goodness Sharon lived to share her story so that others might benefit from it.

Amazon Review

I found this book very interesting and couldn't put it down. As the author's life unfolds she reveals suffering depression through thoughts and experiences in an honest, yet sensitive way that many can relate to. The subject of depression and suicide thoughts should be dealt with more openly, not alone, and this encounter should be read.

Amazon Review

This book really helped me understand the mindset of someone whose mental illness would lead her to attempt to take her own life. Sixty-ninth Street Suicide is compelling and a fast read.

Amazon Review

It was insightful and could not put it down. Thank you for wearing your emotions on your sleeve - its a learning experience for all. I highly recommend this book to all!

Amazon Review

It's so complicated and difficult to explain the unexplainable. For those who happen to be the one struggling with depression/anxiety or self-harm or if you have a friend or loved one who is, this book is for you. So much of Sharon's story was my story, I could relate with much of her story. Reading the book was therapeutic for me on many levels.

Amazon Review

Sixty-ninth Street
Suicide

"Hardships often prepare ordinary people for an extraordinary destination."

C.S. Lewis

Dedicated to all those who have tragically committed suicide. On behalf of you, I share my story to help the world understand mental illness and end the stigma that prevents too many from seeking help.

Ryan Reid • Steve Cash • Robin Williams • Anthony Bourdain • Kate Spade • Freddy Prinz • David Swain • Ashley Mattingly • Stuart Adamson • John Mondello • Lorna Breen • Sophie Gradon • Ahn Jae-hwan • Mike Thalassitis • Caroline Flack • Pavle Jovanovic • Jeremy M. Jordan • Jas Waters • Shay Razaei • Chantal Akerman • Sulli • Leelah Alcorn • Goo Hara • Cha In-Ha • Tony Cook • Alexander E. Kearns • Steven Bing • Alan Kirschenbaum • Byron Bernstein • Nancy Motes • Mike Awesome • Robert Fuller • Siya Kakkar • Sushant Singh Rajput • Master Sgt. Andrew Christian Marckesano • Ashley Massaro • Benjamin Keough • August Ames • Steve Phillip • Gia Allemand • Julian • Deputy Chief Dion Boyd • Desmond Amofah • Sgt. Linhong Li • Johnny Rios • Robert Echeverria • Steven Silks • Chris Acland • Stephanie Adams • Ekaterina Alexandrovskaya • Avicii • Pratyusha Banerjee • Johanna Bassani • Ari Behn • Chester Bennington • David Berman • Molly Brodak • Simone Battle • Jadin Bell • Helena Belmonte • Malik Bendjelloul • Tim Bergling • Paul Bhattacharjee • Bob Birch • Jeremy Blake • Isabella Blow • Eduardo Bonvallet • Jonathan Brandis • Freddy E. Buhl • Katelyn Nicole Davis • Tyler Clementi • Christopher Dorner • Charmaine Dragun • Keith Emerson • Robert Enke • Fausto Fanti • Mark Fisher • Keith Flint • Goo Ha-ra • Spalding Gray • Charles Haddon • Ryan Halligan • Choi Jin-ri • David Kellermann • Margot Kidder • Kim Jonghyun • Hana Kimura • Dave Lepard • Arnie Lerma • Harry Lew • Keith Andes • David Buckel • Brad Bufanda • Brian Christopher • Bernard Loiseau • Roman Lyashenko • Ellen Joyce Loo • Chris Cornell • John Coughlin • Keith Emerson • Caroline Flack • Kelly Fraser • Jason Hairston • Sarah Hegazi • Victor Heringer • Nikki Bacharach • Jill Janus • John B. McLemore • Alexander McQueen • Megan Meier • Jill Messick • Ambrose Olsen • Ali-Reza Pahlavi • Darrin Patrick • Phoebe Prince • Todd Reid • David Reimer • Ellie Soutter • Deon Stewardson • Brian Velasco • Jeon Mi-seon • Atsumi Yoshikubo • Dan Johnson • Greg Johnson • Pavle Jovanonic • Margot Kidder • Stan Kirsch • Billy Knight • Paul Lambert • Ellen Joyce Loo • Bhaiyyu Maharaj • Michael Mantenuto • Jill Messick • Flávio Migliaccio • Dave Mirra • Tommy Page • Mico Palanca • Kushal Punjabi • Byron Daniel Bernstein • John Rheinecker • Stevie Ryan • Oksana Shachko • Scott Stearney • Jean Stein • Steve Stephens • Jon Paul Steuer • Brody Stevens • Choi Jin-ri • Adam Svoboda • Mike Thalassitis • Verne Troyer • Jarrid Wilson • Stephen Wooldridge • Yang Yang • Jill Messick • Llyr George • Daisy Coleman • Audrie Pott • Sameer Sharma • Kirsty Bonner • Landon Clifford • Brian Love • Jim Curyn • Evan Loh • Lance Corporal Nicholas Rodriguez • Patrick John P.J. Donovan • Tysen Benz • Von Mercado • Phillip Spruill • Ronnie McNutt • Loren Grey • Chase Hudson • Addison Rae • Enkyboy • Charli d' amelio • Daisy Keech • Lex • Mads • Tayler Holder • Nancy Motes • Randi Kaye's father

Chapter 1

Wake-Up Call

From the age of seventeen, it was always in the back of my mind that one day I'd kill myself. It wasn't until thirty-six years later that I acted on this thought. But I never considered what would happen if I survived. After five days in a coma from overdosing on two hundred Xanax pills, I discovered two revelations. I was in the throes of depression, and I was labeled a serious suicide risk because I'd consumed enough pills to die. When my life didn't end, a new one began. This is my story from birth to rebirth.

For the last six days, I haven't heard a sound or had a single dream. My coma has held me hostage in pure blackness, which is an appropriate way to end what has been the darkest chapter in my life. But I don't know this yet because I'm still lying unconscious in the ICU while my family sits vigil by my bedside. After I develop pneumonia from the intubation tube, everyone has been told that there are three possible outcomes: I might wake up and be fine, wake up with permanent disabilities or never wake up at all. I finally show signs of life as my left arm begins moving on day four. But I don't move my right side, which is cause for concern. The doctors are worried that I had a stroke. I didn't. As I slowly begin gaining consciousness, it feels like someone is dragging me out of a deep sleep. It reminds me of times when I've been snoozing, but I'm still aware of my surroundings. I don't want to wake up, but I feel completely powerless to fight whatever is pulling me back to life. I'm pretty sure that I'm not alone, but I can't open my eyes to look around. My weak body also refuses to move, no matter how hard I try. Suddenly, my mom's high-pitched voice breaks through the darkness. I can detect an edge of desperation as she urgently encourages me, "Sharon, Sharon, it's OK, open your eyes." Why does it seem like she's speaking through a tube from the other end of the room? I can't look to see where I am or if my mother is really here because my eyelids still feel as though they're cemented shut.

Every time my brain temporarily awakens, I'm jarred by a searing pain in my throat. It's all that I can focus on. Adding to, or causing the pain, is blasting air that's being forced down my windpipe. With each swallow, it feels as if something is scraping my throat with sandpaper. Suddenly, it occurs to me that I might be waking up with a bad case of strep. I haven't felt throbbing pain like this since having my tonsils removed in the eleventh grade. With each intake of air, I hear the hissing of a machine that sounds like the ones I've seen on my beloved medical TV shows. But it never occurs to me to question why I'm attached to a breathing machine that is only used for the sickest of patients. Its blip warns me every time that my throat is about to be set on fire. The regularity leaves me in a heightened state of anticipation. I'm irrationally struggling not to swallow and failing miserably.

Suddenly, I realize that a massive thick pipe about the width of a silver dollar is clogging my throat. Putting everything together, I assume that this is what has been blowing me up like a helium balloon every few seconds. How long has it been here? Does anyone realize that it feels like a form of torture? Somehow, I know it's dangerous to touch whatever this mysterious object is. Instead, I raise up my left arm from the elbow in slow motion to point and pray that someone reads my mind. But everyone completely misreads my hand signal and admonishes me in unison, "No, no, put your hand down, don't pull it out." While my mom tightly grasps my fingers in case I don't get the message, my mind silently screams, "Get your hands off of me, I'm not trying to yank it out." If there was any way to shoot her a dirty look, I would. But my eyes still have a mind of their own and remain tightly shut. When they finally decide to open for longer than two seconds, it feels as if someone has turned on a nightlight in my brain. My peripheral vision has all but disappeared, and I can only see about five inches in front of my face.

Is that Springsteen I hear in the distance belting out "Thunder Road?" No wait, it's "Born to Run," the song that made me fall in love with his raspy voice to the point of obsession. The music is loud and annoying as I try gaining clarity—I wish someone would shut it off. But I instinctively know that I can't talk, and I don't bother trying. After what feels like an eternity but is probably just a few minutes, I find the strength to slowly flutter open my eyelids. I can only squint because it feels like I'm staring straight into the blazing rays of the midday sun. My mom's face is surrounded by a black fog that makes it seem like she's floating in space. All I can focus on is her short curly red hair that makes her pale skin look translucent. She begins enthusiastically coaching me, "That's it, you're doing a great job," the same way she once encouraged my daughter Morgan to drink from the big girl cup. Her face is oddly elongated as if she's used one of those iPhone face apps to purposely distort it.

Springsteen's music is blaring from my right. It's making my head pound because, unbeknownst to me, I'm slowly awakening from a coma. "Please shut it off," I beg, but no one can hear my silent plea. Gradually, I regain my peripheral vision and can keep my eyes open for slightly longer amounts of time. That's when I catch a glimpse of my sister's husband Tom lurking in the background. He looks composed and completely out of place in contrast to everyone else, whose wide-eyed expressions appear as if they have been watching the world come to an end. If I was thinking straight, I'd probably wonder why my ex-husband Ed and the kids aren't around. I later learn that this is the first day they haven't been holed up in the hospital, waiting for me to either wake up or die. I find out later that they desperately needed a break and stayed home but hopped back in the car as soon as my sister informed them that I'm awake.

After gently turning my head to the right, I catch Alyce standing over my bed. She's holding something close to my ear. Suddenly, I realize that the music has been coming from her iPad. She doesn't understand how it has been annoying the hell out of me from the moment I began gaining consciousness. Now that I know where Bruce's sexy, but way-too-loud, voice has been serenading me from, I visualize hitting the iPad's off button. If I had the energy and control to swat it away, it would fly across the room and smash against the wall. Everything in this never-ending dream is sending my senses into a frenzy. I'm super irritated. I later learn that my sister has been playing Bruce's music for the past two days. She knew that if anyone could rouse me up from a coma, it's the Boss. When Alyce abruptly bends over and whispers, "Do you want me to continue playing the music?" I shake my head in slow motion. Bruce is finally silenced with the click of the off button.

I'm pretty sure that my friend Melanie, who recently moved back to her hometown of Kansas City, is sitting to my left. She and my mom are rubbing the tops of my veiny warm hands. It's how I imagine comforting an elderly person in a nursing home. When I tune into her cute Midwestern accent, I'm convinced that she's not a figment of my currently warped imagination. From straight ahead, my mom's face continues to loom over me and now seems real—she no longer looks distorted or reminds me of Salvador Dali's melting clock. Why is there tremendous sadness in her eyes and a gentle kindness in her voice? Her continued pleading for me to remain awake becomes my focal point as she slowly brings me into the world for a second time. It takes a while to gain my bearings. Since I'm solely focused on what's within my line of vision, I don't realize that a nurse is sitting in the room. Or that I'm hooked up to a machine that makes my head look like an overloaded electrical socket.

As I become more coherent, I still can't speak with what I've now been informed is an intubation tube. It's been pushing air into my lungs and breathing life into my comatose body for the past five days. My mom further explains that the same tube that kept me alive almost killed me by causing pneumonia. To protect me, she hides the fact that I've been in a coma. Only when Ed shows up do I learn the gritty details. As my foggy head tries to digest the bits and pieces of information that I've been given, I conclude that this isn't a dream—it's a living nightmare. And right now, everything sucks. My family has been warned by the floor nurse, "Many survivors wake up angry after they realize they were saved against their will." While I can't recall when or how I was reminded that suicide had brought me to this dark place, rage never once crosses my mind. Sadness replaces confusion as I realize that I'm the cause of everyone's obvious turmoil and emotional agony. At some point, my mom assures me, "You'll be OK. You're depressed, and we'll get you the help you need." A light bulb goes off in my head. As I lay in my hospital bed, hooked up to all kinds of machines that have kept me alive for the past few days, I feel hope for the first time in ten years. My body is frail, but my determination grows stronger by the hour. Depression has been lying to me for the past ten years, convincing me that I'll never be happy again. This enlightenment is the first step in overpowering my demons. A huge wave of relief washes over me once I comprehend that I'm not destined to be miserable forever. I never thought that I'd be blessed with a second chance—or ever want one.

After making it clear through hand signals that I want to communicate, my sister holds up her iPad and suggests, "You can write a message on here." But my bumbling fingers and dizzy brain aren't ready to work in unison and can't hit a single letter. "Is this permanent," I wonder with panic building, "Can I no longer write or spell?" Alyce comes up with the brilliant idea of playing a modified version of charades. Before we begin, she instructs, "I'll go through the alphabet, and you signal when I get to the correct letter." Her tightly pursed lips reveal her frustration when she has to go through almost all twenty-six options. When she asks if it's a vowel, and I give a thumbs up, she does a little happy dance. Everyone else is acting like this is a game. My mom is making spastic hand signals as if she can mystically pull the sentence out of my head. Tom is getting ahead of Alyce, who is slowly going through the alphabet and confusing her. Her expression is priceless. The first sentence that I begin spelling out is, "I'm sorry." But before I can get to the second "r," Alyce places her hand on top of mine and says, "Don't ever apologize. We're just glad you're alive." I vaguely recall then falling back into temporary unconsciousness before having the chance to communicate anything else.

A thin, itchy blanket is pulled all the way up to my neck. It's making me miserably warm and sweaty. I desperately want to toss it off but removing it by myself seems as likely as walking out of the hospital this minute on my own two feet. I use all my energy to kick it off and hope that my legs cooperate. They do, but much to my chagrin, my mom immediately places the blanket back on. I'm unable to keep my eyes open long enough to shoot her an exasperated look that says, "Stop it, I'm hot." Instead, I kick higher and higher in the hope that she takes the hint. After about the fourth frustrating time, I toss up the blanket so high that it goes flying over the bed's protective metal guard rail. I'm naked underneath, so everyone in the room now knows exactly what my thin, pale white body looks like. My mom finally gets the message as I hear her exclaim, "I guess she doesn't want the blanket on her." But as Alyce later informs me, "You gave everyone quite a show, including Tom."

That afternoon, or it might've been late morning, "I heard you're awake," announces the arrival of three cheery doctors in long, white hospital coats. The stethoscopes loosely placed around their necks hang down like pieces of jewelry. There are two men who look to be in their late thirties and a younger attractive woman with mesmerizing blue eyes and black hair. The head doctor's straight posture and somewhat formal tone informs me that he's in charge. He diligently glances over the chart that has been recording my every move—and non-move—for the past few days. As he begins reading my stats out loud, the other two doctors nod in agreement. Once again, I point to the enemy down my throat while hoping that a professional can read sign language better than my family. Dr. Mark immediately calms me down with his reassuring baritone voice. "I know it's uncomfortable, and I promise we'll remove it this afternoon. If you can breathe on your own, it's out for good." I slowly put up my right thumb as a sign of approval. My mom immediately begins playing twenty questions with the busy doctor, who quickly and successfully cuts her off by announcing, "We'll be back around four o'clock to remove the intubation tube and answer any questions you may have. Until we know she can breathe on her own, it's impossible to know her status." My squinty eyes wander left as I watch the doctors depart through my room's glass door to visit other patients in the ICU on the brink of death. It's now a waiting game as I anticipate their return to relieve me of what has, so far, been the most painful part of this atrocious journey. As my fuzzy mind and stiff body slowly come back to life from its long unnatural slumber, I now understand what a bear must feel like upon awakening from a six-month hibernation.

Some peace and quiet would be nice while my brain takes its time rejoining the world. So, I'm beyond pleased when everyone mercifully leaves the room to grab something to eat in the downstairs cafeteria. The day nurse sitting next to me can now focus on my needs without interruption from my well-intentioned but nonetheless overbearing family. When she asks what she can do for me, I gesture to my back. She gently adjusts my pillows to better support my head, which is making me feel like I'm on a never-ending roller coaster. She then shifts my blanket so that I don't accidentally pull out the IV in my left arm. After sitting back down, she takes it upon herself to leisurely massage my hands and arms with a fruity smelling lotion that someone must've brought to the hospital. I'm beginning to feel the tiniest bit better as I slowly shake off the effects of the coma. But I try laying perfectly still. Any movement adds ammunition to a budding migraine that will soon torture me for weeks to come.

Right on time, the same doctors from the morning work their way to my bed. Everyone moves to either corner of the small room.

It happens instantaneously and reminds me of Moses parting the Red Sea in *The Ten Commandments*. The female doctor hooks up what she explains is a carbon monoxide machine. "It'll monitor your output to ensure that your breathing is normal." I watch, fascinated, as she hangs a small, white box on my IV pole. It reminds me of the universal adapter I take on vacations overseas. Everyone holds their breath as the doctor carefully slides out the thick, clear tube. It feels like she's pulling a clown's never-ending chain of colorful hankies out of my mouth. As the last of the tube is removed, I now have room to gag from the pneumonia. I sound like an angry quacking duck while suffering an uncontrollable coughing fit for the next two minutes. But everyone breathes a sigh of relief as I inhale and exhale on my own. When I try speaking for the first time, the only noise that comes out sounds like a whispering Minnie Mouse. This frustrates me because I have so many unanswered questions. The doctor assures me, "Your voice will come back. You probably burnt your throat when you aspirated." Everyone now has to listen carefully if they have any chance of hearing what I have to say. Eventually, I'm told to stop talking and give my throat the time that it needs to heal.

Suddenly, I catch sight of Ed, Pam and the children lined up by my bed. They're seemingly frozen in fear and all intently staring at me. My foggy brain hasn't processed everything yet. So, I have no knowledge that they've been in my room for the past few days, willing me to open my eyes. I'm hellbent on protecting my sensitive son Myles, who is standing directly in my line of vision. I lie and whisper, "I have pneumonia. That's what almost killed me." He looks at me sideways, which I later learn is because he's been a part of this unfortunate journey the entire time. Ed pulls him aside and advises, "Just go along with whatever mommy says." But the children know that I intentionally tried to kill myself, and there's no sense in trying to sugarcoat the truth. Never one to mince words, Ed takes it upon himself to lay out the truth. Toward the end of the visit, he asks, "Do you know what day it is?" I guess, "Tuesday or Wednesday," since I'm pretty sure that I overdosed on a

Monday. Ed shakes his head and says, "No, it's Sunday. You've been in a coma for five days." This shocking revelation adds perspective as I try unraveling my current predicament.

Chapter 2

Growing Up

Too many people asked me, "Why don't you smile?" Silently, I responded, "I don't know. Why don't you fuck off?"

I'll admit it, I've never been able to smile without looking like a chimpanzee in heat. That's probably why I'm drawn to people who radiate happiness with their pearly whites. I've always found their obvious joy as contagious as sneezing. Don't get me wrong. Smile or no smile, people still considered me pleasing to the eye. I was your typically cute suburban girl with long brown banana curls like Shirley Temple, an average height that peaked at 5'4", high cheekbones, light brown almond-shaped eyes, long legs and a non-stereotypical Jewish button nose. And, of course, a small mouth that wasn't fond of smiling. In most of my baby pictures, I appear deep in thought. But I'm not sure what a six-month-old would have to think about, especially without a vocabulary. When I asked my mom why I looked so serious, she responded, "You pretty much only smiled when you burped." Much to my chagrin, my glum expression becomes a topic of conversation all throughout my life. These days, it's called resting bitch face. When teachers asked, "Sharon, what's wrong?" I responded, "Nothing." But now something did bother me because I'd developed a complex. This added to my awkwardness of being a self-conscious, gangly preteen whose insecurity led to thumb-sucking until the age of ten. My mom, dad and my sister Alyce didn't exactly have killer smiles, either. So, no one in the Appleman family ever look deliriously happy like the Osmond Brothers—and let's not forget Marie. Nonetheless, we were a relatively content bunch—especially compared to some of the dysfunctional families I've seen ripping each other apart on Dr. Phil.

My dad had a big personality with a dry sense of humor, which entered the room five paces ahead of him. I'd never considered him typically handsome because all I could focus on was his huge nose. But I always gazed at him endearingly because, to me, he was pure love. He had a full head of short, black hair, olive skin, deep brown eyes, gapped teeth, a barrel chest, long legs that made him seem taller than 5'10", and that nose that took up a good part of his face. Raised by first-generation humble immigrants, my dad had simple tastes. His favorite piece of clothing was a pair of ripped green army pants that he wore in the military reserves. My mom couldn't stand them. Eventually, she began coordinating spiffy cashmere sweaters with corduroy pants so that he didn't always look like he was ready for active duty. There are two things about him that stand out most. The first is his distinct nose. Second is the way his long legs glided at twenty miles per hour like a typical New Yorker. Whenever my younger self accompanied him to work, my little feet had to scurry if there was any chance of keeping up. When I moved into the city after college, I became a quintessential New Yorker whose regular walking pace was a slow jog.

Almost every day, my dad declared, "You have no idea how much I adore you and your sister." He must've proclaimed his love to us at least a million times and referred to us as his pride and joy. But he couldn't have been more off base because we did know, and we cherished him just as much. It felt safe being loved and adored, as I learned from being *daddy's little girl*. But as I grew older, it made me—dare I say—needy in the emotional department. Whenever my sister was the center of attention, I would dramatically sob, "Nobody loves me." Perhaps I was subconsciously redirecting my parent's focus. As they rushed over to reassure me, I'd immediately throw my arms around my dad's wide chest and wouldn't let go.

The only person I didn't like hugging was my sister—we didn't become close until our late twenties. Alyce had an undiagnosed learning disability and a weight problem. So, who could blame her for resenting a sister like me who brought home practically perfect grades and had an effortlessly trim figure? We were very different people in pretty much every way. When we weren't ignoring each other, we were constantly bickering. While I inherited my dad's long legs and lean body, my sister resembled his short, stocky mother. Alyce was 5'3" with black wavy hair that was always worn short, olive skin, striking green almond-shaped eyes and Grandma's nose (which was wide but much smaller than my dad's). But she was always more patient and less aggressive than I was, so I considered her the kinder daughter. It didn't come as a surprise when she became a special ed teacher while I chose to write in the *prepare to get stabbed in the back* world of advertising.

My mom was my role model and taught me at a young age how to stand up for myself. She was a strong woman who always appeared well put together. Her hair was perfectly coiffed from her weekly Saturday morning beauty parlor primping. Right after her hair appointment, she had her nails professionally polished in either dark pink or some shade of red. Every morning during the week, she spent an hour carefully putting on a full face of tasteful makeup before choosing an outfit that accentuated her curvy figure. Despite being a stay-at-home mother, she was always dressed as if she had somewhere special to go. Her hazel, almond-shaped eyes, small button nose and high cheekbones were showstoppers. But what stands out the most is her silky soft pale skin that rarely saw the sun.

While I developed my mom's strong personality, my dad passed down his dry sense of humor and affectionate demeanor. Comparing potential boyfriends to him didn't bode well since it took a very special suitor to win me over. Since few men were emotionally fit to fulfill my complex needs, it was near impossible finding someone who met my ridiculously high standards. Those high expectations extended to me, which made it a lifelong battle to love myself and accept my imperfections. As a result, a compelling force to be perfect guided many of my life paths. Unfortunately, pursuing unachievable goals often led me down the wrong path. Whether I was putting together a one hundred piece puzzle or taking a test that determined my acceptance to college, I craved approval the same way that a dog lives to please his master. If I didn't do something right, it wasn't uncommon for whatever I was working on to go flying across the room. Playing Monopoly was one of my biggest triggers. My wrath could become so intense that Alyce ran the other way whenever she caught sight of the white rectangular box in my hand.

My dad never uttered the words, "I expect you to be a high achiever," but he may as well have. In my mind, his downturned, thin mouth conveyed it for him. His parents brought their old-fashioned European values with them when they stepped foot on Ellis Island. Jewish children were expected to make their parents proud by studying hard and earning a respectable living. When he became a criminal tax attorney, I imagine his parents couldn't stop kvelling. My dad had those same extraordinarily high expectations for both me and my sister. But her undiagnosed learning disability placed all the pressure for perfect grades on me. I'm not sure if he consciously knew that his pursed lips often betrayed his internal judgment. During one of those rare times when I became frustrated about schoolwork—geometry was a nightmare—my parents denied that I was expected to earn straight A's. I often wonder if some of the pressure might've been self-induced from my young, wildly paranoid imagination. Regardless, I was harder on myself than, from what I've heard, the fear-inducing nuns who reprimand troublemakers with a wooden ruler.

As early as second grade, I viewed a simple, multiple-choice vocabulary quiz as a matter of life and death. So, one year when my dad decided to joke about my report card, it completely backfired. His worst attempt at humor happened the day that I could hardly contain my excitement as I came bouncing through the door to proudly show off nearly perfect grades—with the exception of one A-. He was in rare form as he teased, "Why did you get an A-, what happened?" Tears blurred my eyes as my mom chastised, "Murray, that's not funny. You're upsetting her." I didn't realize that he was joking, and letting down the most important person in my life was never an option. Of course, this unfortunate incident concluded with a twenty-second bear hug. My dad's been gone for twenty-two years. But as clear as day, I can still envision his deep brown eyes creasing at the corner whenever my sister or I made him proud. My heart sang whenever he verbally praised me with his signature line, "You're a chip off the old block."

Being a people-pleasing goody-goody also extended early on to my teachers. I was the annoying know-it-all who could always be found sitting in the front row, frantically waving my hand like Arnold Horshack in the old TV series *Welcome Back, Kotter*. Predictably the teacher would remark, "Sharon, why don't we let someone else answer?" When my class lined up for assembly, I stood as still as a statue while classmates bounced off the walls. If I was assigned a two-page paper, I naturally wrote ten pages in my somewhat legible chicken scratch. Not only did the content need to be perfect, but God forbid if there were any cross-outs. Since computers didn't exist yet, I often went through an entire stack of loose-leaf paper before handing in my work. Even the extreme pain that I endured after having my tonsils removed at eighteen couldn't stand in the way of my finishing a long writing assignment. I was so miserable in the hospital that I kicked the cup of ice chips out of the nurse's hand. But the moment I returned home, there was no time for rest or giving in to the pain. My tunnel vision focused solely on getting the work done. As my teacher fawned over my paper in class the following week, fellow classmates who hadn't even started yet shot daggers at me. Being a people pleaser was always my MO. Whenever I disappointed myself, or someone else, my internal verbal abuse mechanism scolded, "Why did you do that? How could you make such a stupid mistake?"

My mom often uttered, with a sneer and a tiny bit of disgust detectable in her tone, "You have a Type A personality just like your father." She was right, and I considered it a compliment. But while my dad worked his butt off during the week, he ensured a healthy balance by dedicating time for us on weekends. On Saturday mornings, the house was filled with the banging of his thick fingers on the automatic typewriter's keyboard. Every minute or so, I heard the *bing* that announced him hitting *return*. His routine was finishing up paperwork before enjoying time with the family. Most eight-year-olds look forward to Saturday and Sunday simply because they can sleep in. But I anticipated having my dad's full attention. Some of the highlights included visiting my grandparents in Brooklyn and predictably leaving with a glass jar of grandma's sweet homemade pink applesauce. Or piling our plates high with way more food than we could possibly finish at the Oriental Luau's Sunday night all-you-can-eat buffet. My sister and I anticipated dousing the thick, powdered, delicately crunchy noodles in duck sauce before plopping it in our mouths.

While my dad toiled away at work during the week, my mom was stuck with me and Alyce. At least, that's the impression she gave. Our constant bickering drove her crazy. After dealing with squabbling kids of my own, I don't blame her. She also didn't seem thrilled with being responsible for every little thing that pertained to us. Doctor appointments, preparing for a new school year, teacher conferences, carpooling—you name it, and she was in charge. My maternal grandmother worked full-time in the 1970s, and I'd always considered her a career woman who was ahead of her time. My mom was the same way. Having the luxury to build a career would've undoubtedly fulfilled the ambitious part of her that being a full-time mother never could. When Alyce and I were old enough to take care of ourselves, my mom bravely attended college at the age of forty. She was determined to make up for lost time and set a lofty example. But her age worked against her when it came time to finding a job. When she finally landed her dream role in her fifties, she was forced to give it up before long due to extenuating circumstances.

Sixty-ninth Street Suicide

My mom wholeheartedly supported and defended me all throughout my younger years. There was a yin and yang to our complex relationship because of an unpredictable anger that festered just below the surface and caused a tense vibe in the house. It was like the feeling you get when you hesitantly tiptoe into a dark basement to inspect an unfamiliar sound. You're sweating and shivering at the same time because you have no idea what you're about to find. But you're also too petrified to ignore it. It didn't help matters that I'd always absorbed people's energy, both positive and negative. The solution was hiding behind the safety of my closed bedroom door. Before stepping into the house, I always asked myself, "Is the coast clear?" I treaded lightly because I'd never be sure which mood would greet me on any given day. Whenever I spotted my mom in the kitchen—which was right by the side door—I practically held my breath as I tentatively entered. Even if I was greeted with a smile, it wasn't necessarily enjoyable because I was already on edge, ready to defend myself. Something as simple as failing to take a phone message could trigger her ranting and raving for five endless minutes. Even if I was innocent, I was often punished because Alyce's response was like a broken record. "Sharon did it," was my cue to get out of my mom's way. For some reason, she always accepted my sister's word as fact, which I decided was because Alyce was her favorite. She'd make a hasty retreat that warned me of impending doom. Inevitably, she was headed straight to her bedroom at the end of the hall to grab her bristled wooden hairbrush. My reaction was equally predictable. I used this head start to try and escape her uncontrollable wrath by locking myself in the closest room. Not trusting the lock, I held the doorknob and leaned back with all 119 pounds of me.

I was considerably stronger than my mom and held my ground. If I was lucky, she'd calm down and walk away before I slowly poked my head out of the door a few minutes later to assess the situation. On days when she somehow plowed through the door that I was hiding behind, she pounded the brush on my right upper arm with the same frenzy that someone uses when playing Whack-a-Mole. My reaction was to automatically raise my arms to protect my face and cry—out of frustration, not pain. These episodes made me feel unloved because you don't treat someone like this unless you don't like them. Hitting her back never once crossed my mind, probably because I feared pissing her off even more. With each hit of the brush, I saw nothing but hate in her hazel green eyes. I was convinced that she was pummeling me because she wished that I was never born. Her blind rage scared me, especially since it was coming from the woman who also nurtured me. The smacking usually went on for about twenty seconds before she'd storm out of the room and lock herself in her bedroom.

One day, I'd finally reached my breaking point while trying to protect myself from something that I didn't do. My anger now matched my mom's, and it wasn't pretty. As I held the doorknob to the laundry room, my growing frustration prompted me to spontaneously take action and throw open the door. I was met with a bewildered look on my mom's face. I must've had a crazed look of my own because she froze on the spot. Without giving it a second thought, I took a couple of steps forward and kicked her in the shin. I wasn't wearing shoes, but I'd clearly made my point. My mom stared at me wide-eyed as I sternly announced, "I'm older now, and you will never hit me again." She never did. But that frightened little girl still lives inside me today and makes her presence known in the form of paranoia and oversensitivity.

The Right Move

On more than one occasion, I overheard my parents discussing the pros and cons of living in a more diverse neighborhood. I'd hear my mom say, "It's better for the kids to grow up with people of similar backgrounds," while my dad grunted in agreement.

My mom was frustrated by our living situation in a predominantly non-Jewish part of Rockland County. She carpooled with two other mothers to schlep the only three Jewish kids in the neighborhood to Hebrew school a good fifteen minutes away. If I wanted to hang out with someone on the weekend, either my mom or dad was the designated driver because my friends' parents wouldn't go out of their way to take them to my house. They didn't have to. Since most of my friends lived in the next town over, they could easily find someone else nearby to hang out with. On the other hand, I'd get stuck spending the day alone. While my friends were a mix of personalities, all were authentic and nonjudgmental. I wouldn't accept anything less since labeling people has always gone against my open-mindedness. One of my girlfriends had her cancerous leg amputated and wore a wig because of chemo. To me, she was just Carla. Another friend was a little person, but I hung out with her because she had a big personality. "Who am I to judge" is a mantra that I live by to this day. When I was thirteen, my parents sat me and my sister down to announce that we were moving. I was thrilled to make a new start. We packed up the house toward the end of the summer and set down roots in New City, New York—which was more upscale with better schools and Jews galore.

In our old house, everything had its place and needed to look perfect. The plastic on the couch couldn't be wrinkled, the kitchen chairs were pushed in just so and bedspreads were mandated to keep the blanket underneath clean. I fought my mom on the bedspread until she finally gave in as long as my bed was made—which it always was. So, it wasn't surprising that she didn't consider anyone's comfort while decorating our new, white brick ranch home. The tchotchkes were so fragile and off-limits that I didn't even glance in their direction. The kitchen chairs' wooden armrests had to touch the table at a certain angle when they weren't being used. I could deal with all that. But a constant source of frustration was the puffy red couch in the den. It was so mushy that it felt like I was sitting on a pile of bird feathers. Whenever I sunk into it, my butt left an indent. My mom's sixth sense then demanded that she immediately run to the den and fluff the pillows. When I snuck home from school for lunch, she noticed that the cushions weren't perfectly smooth and asked, "Why did you come home during school?" When I questioned how she knew, she pointed to where the couch was in the den and simply stated, "Indents." This was the reason why I predominantly watched TV on my thirteen-inch black and white Panasonic in my bedroom.

Eventually, I began craving my own control to balance out the self-induced stress of seeking perfection. Having everything in its place provided the relief that I deeply yearned for. In my mind, things like desk papers lined up at the same angle helped silence the noise in my head. At least once a week, I could be found joyfully rolling the fifteen-pound blue Hoover from one end of our ranch house to the other. I'm pretty sure that most parents don't arrive home to find their child spontaneously vacuuming the house because "I had the urge." But I'd essentially graduated from being neat to becoming a neat and clean freak. On the other hand, my stubborn father refused to have anything to do with my mom's sterile-as-a-museum environment. In fact, I'm pretty sure that he got a kick out of leaving his papers and files stacked precariously high in the bedroom that he used as his workspace. His office in the city was in equal disarray, and I often jokingly threatened to blow up his filing system with a fan. My parents were stubbornly dysfunctional; my mom usually had the last word because my dad just wanted to make whatever they were arguing about go away. But cleaning his office was one of those rare instances when he wouldn't budge. The compromise was her closing the door every morning to hide the one mess that she could never control.

The grass is always greener on the other side. At least that's what I once believed until wisdom taught me otherwise. So, I considered moving and attending a new school as a once-in-a-lifetime chance for a do-over. In this case, the grass didn't disappoint because moving presented the perfect opportunity for me to clear the slate, reinvent myself and belong to a popular group of friends. Since we left our old house at the end of August, I didn't meet the neighborhood kids until a week later on the first day of school. Fortunately, my mom already knew a couple of our new neighbors before purchasing the house, and their daughters were told to keep an eye out for me. I wasn't sure what to expect as I hesitantly climbed up the five oversized steps that led me straight toward the overweight, scruffy bus driver. The instant that I turned left, five smiling faces in the back seats reserved for the cool kids were waiting to introduce themselves and say hello. Renee, Julie, Carolyn, Lisa and Melissa made me feel welcome from the get-go. Being included in their plans from day one meant that a group had *chosen me*. Belonging to a great set of friends felt as fulfilling as finding an extra five dollars in my pocket at school on pizza day.

My new pals introduced me to a far more exciting and bolder life that, until then, I'd only seen in movies like *Fast Times at Ridgemont High*. About two weeks after meeting everyone, someone passed me a joint while asking, "Wanna take a hit?" I took a deep puff that had me coughing up a lung for a good half a minute. But the soothing rush put me in a deep bliss that instantly birthed a diehard pothead at a mere fourteen years of age. I relied on this newfound relief whenever I wanted to chill out. Smoking also dulled the horrendous migraines that I'd suffered from the early age of seven by gently lifting me to a place higher than the pain. Becoming a pothead at such an influential age was a significantly life-changing event that quickly grew into a large part of my teenage identity. During lunch period at school, our group often munched out on Burger King after getting stoned in my friend Eileen's tomato-red VW Beatle on the drive over. Laughter always drowned out whatever Grateful Dead or Springsteen song was blasting on the radio. When school was done for the day, we often trudged up a busy winding road that was right off our block to hang by the pond. We dodged traffic by walking in a straight line on the roadside dirt path before racing across the street. A sign on the low white fence surrounding the pond warned us not to trespass. But like typical teenagers, we simply climbed over it and pretended that the sign didn't exist. The pond sat in front of a majestic white mini-mansion that would've looked right at home in *Gone with the Wind*. It was surrounded by tall, palm-like trees that provided a soothing cool breeze regardless of how hot the sun was beating. Despite the fact that it was only a few feet off a busy main road, it felt like our own little nirvana.

It was probably curiosity that possessed me to quickly graduate from smoking pot to naively popping any pill that I was offered. It wasn't a result of peer pressure since many of my friends didn't join me on what would sometimes become a bad high. But the first time my friend Shari stuck out a palmful of bright pink pills and asked, "Do you wanna trip?" I grabbed one and popped it into my mouth as if it was a harmless piece of candy. I never had a clue what the pill's effect was supposed to be, and I often ended up praying for the dizziness, nausea or psychedelic madness to go away. My mom always thought it was a migraine that sent me silently lying under a dark blanket, motionless in the fetal position, for twelve hours straight. Drinking was never my thing. The few times when I did catch a buzz, I woke up with a massive migraine that took me out of commission for the entire day. Smoking pot was my way of escaping reality and not feeling like death after the high wore off. It also transformed me into a more outgoing, relaxed Sharon and provided the confidence that I needed to walk right up to a group of peers and join in the conversation. In the past, I would've hiked five minutes out of my way to avoid a crowd—even if I knew at least one person there. But this courage was limited, and social settings like bars and parties still shot my anxiety into overdrive. I was known as the one in the group who was always the first to call it a night when I'd found the nerve to go out at all.

I was probably high around eighty percent of the time. During one of the rare instances when I was straight, my mom exclaimed, "Your pupils are as big as saucers," She had become so used to my squinty red eyes that I only appeared different when I wasn't high. I'm not sure what possessed me to keep my drug stash in the same place, even after she found it during one of her monthly searches. Whenever she confronted me, I looked at her with puppy dog eyes and lied, "It isn't mine, it's a friend's." When she once maintained that she had one of my pills tested at a lab, I asked her what it was. She wasn't the only one who wanted to be enlightened—I knew as little about the pill as she did. We now laugh together while reminiscing about the crap that I pulled. My mom couldn't deal if the couch pillows weren't fluffed, but she tolerated my drug bullshit all throughout high school because, as she says, "I tried every way I could to make you stop, but nothing worked."

Pleasing my dad took precedence over everything else. If getting high had prevented me from maintaining my straight-A average, I would've stopped immediately. He convinced himself that his little angel couldn't possibly be using drugs if I consistently brought home top grades. Seeing me through gold-colored lenses always made disappointing him all the more tragic.

My constant pot smoking allowed the authentic part of Sharon to blossom. If we hadn't moved, I'm pretty sure that I wouldn't have morphed into the quirky tell-it-like-it-is person I am today. And I like her.

Chapter 3

Defining the Beginning of My Why

Jealousy rose in me whenever friends spoke about their positive first-time sexual experiences. Mine was so disturbing that it triggered my first depressive episode.

I was sixteen when I met Larry on a cross-country teen tour. Although he was with a different group, we shared a couple of nights together at the same campground. When the two groups sat together for a meal of burnt hot dogs and hamburgers, I had to catch my breath. Staring back from across the long wooden picnic table was a guy who looked like a blonde-haired, blue-eyed model from a Land's End catalog. Being innocent at the time, Larry and I did nothing more than make out in the empty baggage compartments underneath the bus—along with several other teens and counselors. Those two extraordinary days were the highlight of my summer, and the fact that Larry was an Adonis made it all the sweeter. Before our tours went their separate ways, Larry scratched his home number in my notepad (there were no cell phones at the time) and made me promise to call when I returned home.

We reconnected my first week back in New York. On weekends he drove forty minutes from Westchester to my home in Rockland County, honking his horn to announce his arrival. At our young age, living twenty-five miles apart was considered a long-distance relationship.

When my parents were going away for the weekend, we immediately made plans to hang out at my house and knew what that meant. I was looking forward to losing my virginity and seeing what all the fuss was about because asking someone to describe sex is as easy as articulating the love that a mother has for her child. And the closest I'd ever come to anything that resembled intimacy up to that point was watching boys' reactions to *Playboy* magazine and *Victoria's Secret* catalog. After a couple of my friends lost their virginity, I was determined to join the club. The sex was a lot of fumbling and groping—exactly what you'd expect from an inexperienced sixteen-year-old boy. But my expectations were pretty low as I entered this new territory. I had no regrets and was sure that this once-in-a-lifetime first experience would bring us closer as a couple.

When Larry cut out a few hours later, he gave me his usual smooch goodbye. But then he seemingly disappeared. When my patience ran dry a week later, I finally caved in and called him. During our brisk conversation, he nonchalantly mentioned that he didn't want a long-distance relationship. In other words, he planned all along on taking my virginity before dumping me. Larry's insensitivity killed my one chance at having the dreamy kind of experience that I'd read about in corny romance novels. In my mind, he was supposed to whisk me off my feet and adore me like my father did. His using me before dumping me came as a terrible shock. The sex was memorable for all the wrong reasons and summoned a sadness that I'd never known before.

This was the first time that my demons dragged me to a dark, forbidden place I'd soon come to know all too well. It was also the origin of an overwhelming conviction, and lifelong fear, that I'd remain single and alone for the rest of my life. Since I've never been able to hide my emotions, my mom knew that something was up. She kept pestering me to *share my pain*. But despite her always being supportive, spilling the truth seemed impossible. What was I going to say? "Larry used me because he wanted to take my virginity, and now that he's broken up with me, I'm in unbearable pain?" I don't recall how I snapped out of it, but the depression eventually subsided on its own. Thankfully, I didn't allow this dreadful experience to spoil future intimacy.

Pregnancy and Punishment

I'm only seventeen, and I think I'm pregnant. This made my first experience with Larry seem like a day at the beach.

Randy and I were introduced at a party during my junior year of high school and his first year in college. His thick lips, longish black hair and lightly bearded chin immediately caught my eye. On weekends, when he drove up from southern New Jersey, nausea from anticipation prevented me from partaking in the family's ritual Friday night Shabbat dinner. In retrospect, the relationship was built on mutual chemistry and not much else. While getting caught up in the romance of going out with someone in college—and dating in general—I overlooked glaring flaws, including Randy's lack of affection. After our breakup, I discovered that he was dating, and most likely sleeping with, other women at school. This added to the agonizing heartache that was about to unfold. I didn't realize that I ovulate around the seventeenth day of my period, not the fourteenth day. Regardless, it was beyond irresponsible not using protection on one of our weekends together. Panic set in when I missed my period, which normally arrived like clockwork. My heart sank when I knew that the double blue line on the pregnancy test would change my life forever. Having a baby at seventeen never once occurred to me. I was too emotionally immature to consider anything other than an abortion and made the monumental decision without giving it enough thought. It's a mistake that quickly came back to bite me in the ass. Randy's reaction was both unexpected and shocking as he raged in front of our friends with a venom that terrified me. Spit came flying out of both sides of his mouth as he shrieked, "You wanted this, you got pregnant on purpose." He walked away from the situation and refused to take me for the procedure. All at once, overwhelming despair, anger, fright and helplessness held me in its grip. The coward never looked back as he quickly grabbed his keys and left—maintaining his stride as he snatched his black leather jacket off the back of the sofa on the way out. I berated myself for not only getting into this horrific situation but fooling myself that Randy liked me for more than just sex. After his tirade, there was nothing I wanted more than to avoid friends' questioning looks. So, I watched Randy's car from the front window and bolted out of the house the second I saw the bright red taillights on his Buick turn the corner. Unbeknownst to me at the time, screwing up and disappointing myself this badly would permanently kill any chance of achieving *happy Sharon*. It also prohibited me from ever getting to the point where I could completely love myself. Contrary, it set the foundation for never-ending self-hatred. I now considered myself a murderer who deserved nothing but pain and punishment. But it was a subconscious guilt, and I initially couldn't understand why I felt more at peace when my life was empty and lonely. Later, I realized that the emotional pain ensured that I was paying my dues for the worst mistake I'd ever make.

The day after discovering my pregnancy, I kept plans to visit my sister at college in Maryland. Sitting in a *People's Express* aisle seat, I pushed in my flat stomach while begging my period to erase this nightmare. If it did, I promised the universe that I'd never have unprotected sex again. Unfortunately, I was never given the chance to keep my promise. Not being close to my sister at the time, I didn't share my predicament. Instead, I suffered in silence while unsuccessfully trying to convince myself that the pregnancy test was a false positive. I now held my breath every time I used the bathroom, praying to see the tiniest hint of blood. Throughout the weekend, I alleviated stress through nervous eating and the habit of picking my finger. Here began my lifelong battle with food to subconsciously push down insufferable feelings. Upon my return home, I made an appointment at Planned Parenthood to take care of the situation ASAP. The abortion was scheduled for the Monday of President's Day weekend. Unexpectedly, my boss Steve from my part-time job at the deli called that morning, "Hey Sharon, I have something to do. Would you mind covering for me?" My mom overheard the conversation and wouldn't stop nagging, "Why can't you go, Steve needs you to cover for him. I don't understand why you can't do him this favor." Panicked and at a loss for words, the only excuse that came to mind was, "I'm taking my friend for an abortion." It was the early 1980s, when fewer options for birth control meant many women relied on the pull out method—which wasn't terribly effective. My mom initially believed my lie, but I think it's because she desperately wanted to. Her intuition had zero doubt that the abortion was mine. Planned Parenthood didn't allow surgical patients to drive themselves home, so my good friend Eileen accompanied me. On the twenty-minute drive over, I refused to acknowledge that I was about to abort a real baby. Since I was only seven weeks pregnant, there were no symptoms or weight gain to remind me that a living soul was growing inside of me. Upon arrival, a woman at the front desk had me sign in before handing over forms that asked questions like when was my last period and was I having the abortion under duress. Then it was off to the changing room to put on a blue gown, opening in the back. As I waited to be called, I couldn't help but notice that all the other patients were around my age. I thought about how stupid we all were to find ourselves in this predicament. When I awoke from the procedure, the tiniest bit of cramping welcomed my return back to my seemingly normal life. What I didn't know at the time was that my life would never be the same again. After getting dressed, my friend and I stopped at the diner to grab something to eat. At the time, everything I did was mechanical and matter of fact. Emotional numbing enabled me to handle the abortion as nonchalantly as if I'd gone to a dentist appointment. Much to my dismay, Randy didn't pay for the procedure or call afterward to see how I was feeling. I only allowed myself to feel relief, but I all-too-soon discovered that my demons had their own agenda.

    The following weekend, my parents had planned to go on a sightseeing trip to Pennsylvania with their friends. They were under the impression that I was going to attend a teen tour reunion forty minutes away on Long Island. But my intention was enjoying some much-needed time alone. My mom's suspicion went into overdrive when I left the house for a few hours during the time when I should've been packing. Upon arriving home after hanging out with some friends, I nearly tripped over the little brown suitcase that she'd left right outside of my room. Her message was loud and clear—she knew that I had no intention of attending the reunion. But I disregarded her passive/aggressive message and carried on as if there was nothing to worry about. At around nine o'clock, the phone rang with a collect call, but I couldn't hear who it was from. I'll never understand why I picked up the phone when I wasn't supposed to be home. My dad often received business calls, so I talked myself into believing that it wasn't my parents. Years later, my mom told me, "My inner voice didn't let me sleep more than two hours that night."

The following morning, my nightmare was prolonged when I heard a key quickly turning in the side door by the garage. I could practically hear my heart beating out of my chest as I tiptoed across the bedroom to cautiously stick my head out the door. Despite undoubtedly knowing who it was, I prayed with all my might that I was being paranoid. Both parents rushed in with eyes blazing as if they were expecting to find me mid-orgy on their king-sized bed. Little did they know that discovering me having sex would've been a relief compared to what was about to go down. Since my mom was convinced that I stayed home for nonstop lust all weekend, she stormed into my room and gave my tiny private bathroom a once-over. She chased after me while I screamed at the top of my lungs that I just wanted to be alone, which was the truth. I've blocked out any of the other details about our argument until she seemingly shrieked out of nowhere, "The abortion was probably yours!" I was shocked but somewhat relieved to share my dirty secret. Through blinding tears and a runny nose that I unconsciously wiped on the sleeve of my gray sweatshirt, I hesitantly nodded. On my dad's normally loving face was now a look of sheer disgust, one that I'd never witnessed before. His eyes squinted as if they were looking right through me, and his thin lips curled. He seemed blinded by pure hatred as if he was confronting his mortal enemy. This vile rejection terrified me and stole my very last piece of innocence. Without a word, he grabbed his car keys before darting out the side door to collect his thoughts on a long drive to nowhere. My mom tried comforting me as I threw myself on the bed and wailed, "Daddy hates me! He'll never love me again." Upon his return, two hours later, my heart sank when his heavy footsteps hurried past my bedroom. Tears welled up when he didn't stop in to offer the reassurance that I so desperately needed. While placing my ear to my closed bedroom door, I could hear my mom coaxing him, "Murray, she's devastated and needs to know you love her." But it was impossible to register his whispered response. After what seemed like an eternity, my dad took me into his long-outstretched arms and assured me, "Nothing can stop me from loving my little girl." But I didn't buy it, not for one second. I knew without a doubt that given his old-fashioned values, he now viewed the little girl he once adored as a morally corrupt degenerate. He didn't believe in divorce, so I can only imagine what he thought of my having an abortion. I was more upset about hurting the man I adored than the baby whom I'd just callously aborted.

    Severe depression quickly swooped in and brought with it an unbearable anguish. Anyone in my situation would've been upset. But I sobbed nonstop for weeks while coming up with the best way to kill myself. My search always led me back to overdosing, which seemed painless. Staring at the medicine cabinet, I summoned unattainable courage to swallow all my pills and stop the emotional agony. *This became the pivotal moment when I made a pact with my demons to end my life as soon as it became too emotionally intolerable.* Unnerved by a grief that they'd never witnessed before, my parents kept a watchful eye on me 24/7. The sadness slowly retreated with time and by devouring everything in sight. While pigging out somewhat successfully helped me feel nothing, it also packed unwanted pounds onto my normally slim frame. The abortion set the stage for my serious suicide attempt decades later. I'd turned into an immoral lowlife who deserved to die unhappy and unloved. But I didn't immediately acknowledge the demons that had taken permanent residency in my mind. They were accompanied by suicidal thoughts that became as natural as tears wetting my cheeks whenever I watched a tearjerker movie. It was never a question of *if* I'd kill myself one day; it became a matter of *when*. Knowing that I always had an out became my crutch.

For decades, I'd desperately craved closure from Randy. In 2015, I found his email address and sent him a message online. Not only did he write back, but to my amazement, he picked up the phone. Apologetically, he admitted that he'd handled the situation poorly and thought about the baby from time to time. I'd dreamt about hearing those words for decades. Both of us needed to remember this creation, who never had a chance at the life he or she deserved. I often wonder if this child's soul is with my dad in heaven, waiting to reunite with me one day. It's the reason that I'm both pro-life and pro-choice—and confused as hell.

Chapter 4

Eating and Disorder

The instant my fingers grab the cold metal doorknob to enter the side door, my sister's piercing scream startles me, "Get out of my room, I don't want to talk to you." But it doesn't scare me or even surprise me once I take a moment to gather my thoughts. It's time for Mom's and Alyce's monthly smackdown—and I want no part of it. In an attempt to go unnoticed, I tiptoe into the house, softly place my shoes on the beige straw mat by the door and make a beeline to my bedroom. After gently shutting the door behind me, I'm relieved to discover that no one knows I'm home.

    About once a month, we could count on my mom flipping out about something. There was no stopping her until the anger ran its course. When she wasn't going after me about getting high, my sister's closet eating was her biggest trigger. Alyce couldn't manage her eating. My mom was a control freak. Needless to say, this unhealthy dynamic caused most of their shouting matches. Whenever she inspected underneath my sister's bed, potato chip, chocolate and other wrappers could be found shoved in the far corner against the wall. For some reason, Alyce hid the evidence under her bed as predictably as I stowed my pot stash in my middle drawer. Her closet eating must've hit my mom's last nerve because she was as obsessed with my sister's weight as Alyce was fixated on food. It was an unnerving situation that I got pulled into by taking her message to heart that, "You can't be happy if you're fat." Alyce put me down every chance that she got when we were young, and I couldn't understand why. Decades later, she explained, "It felt like you were flaunting your body." In retrospect, I was just being a typical teenager who wore formfitting outfits in an attempt to get noticed. But after the abortion, an extra ten pounds made its presence known in the form of love handles spilling over the sides of my Jordache jeans. I was now an average weight, but I was disgusted with my new fuller figure. Since I'm not one of those people who can devour a large amount of food in one sitting, the weight crept up slowly. It didn't help matters that I worked part-time at a kosher deli, where I was welcome to help myself to everything from the steaming egg barley with a hint of butter to mouthwatering crispy fried chicken. By the time I'd arrive home for dinner, I couldn't eat another bite.

The number on the scale now determined if I had a good or bad day. I wasn't ready to stop emotionally eating until the day that my ex-boyfriend rudely shouted in front of his buddies, "Hey Appleman, did you get fat?" I must've really looked heavy if Graham noticed the change in my body. Feeling absolutely mortified is all the incentive I needed to get this problem under control. I immediately joined a women's Weight Watchers group for the summer. My eating routine now included scrutinizing meals as closely and carefully as diabetics monitor their insulin. This marked the last time that I'd regard food like a normal person ever again. Every time the leader announced our weekly weight loss, the women's applause challenged me to lose even more. By the end of the summer, I'd slimmed down from 130 to 115 pounds. But I still saw an overweight girl looking back at me in the mirror. Once, while my sister and I were out shopping, the saleswoman commented, "You have such a beautiful figure." But I argued—and truly believed—that I still needed to lose weight. Both of them looked at me with distaste before making a beeline to another part of the store to avoid what was sure to be an asinine conversation.

Sixty-ninth Street Suicide

As I was getting ready to leave for Boston University, everyone messed with my head by warning, "You better resist that midnight pizza, or you'll gain the freshman fifteen." That seemed even more petrifying than catching an incurable case of herpes. Like any paranoid girl who's beginning to form an eating disorder would do, I swung in the opposite direction and almost gave up eating altogether. To quell my hunger, I ate four hundred calories of granola and drank four or five cups of tea. The caffeine unintentionally hurt my stomach and added a ten-minute bathroom break to every meal. In my sick mind, diarrhea was another way to lose weight. I satisfied the urge to chew by chomping through three packs of Bubble Yum every day. By the end of the evening, a sea of purple wrappers loaded my garbage pail. I later learned that it's common for anorexics to substitute food with gum to satisfy their urge to chew. Bubble Yum is the equivalent of four sticks of regular gum, and each piece gave my jaw and teeth a hearty workout. Purchasing a few packs in one place became embarrassing—probably because I knew that they wouldn't last the night. But I'm now sure that the student cashier wouldn't have cared less if I'd bought out the store's entire inventory of gum. When I began wasting precious free time purchasing single packs at several stores around campus, I realized that chewing gum had morphed into an addiction. A year later, hypnosis helped me quit the habit and save thousands of dollars on dental work. Controlling every calorie put my exhausting battle with overeating on hold and appeased my neurosis. I felt wanted every time that I caught an attractive man taking a double take of my size two body. Once, I couldn't help but notice my hallmate's friend spin his head around like the exorcist while passing by. She punched him on the arm and teased, "I saw you looking at Sharon. Like what you see?"

There were many things that I enjoyed during college despite my years of eating disorder hell. I laughed a lot with new friends, dated my share of men (but nothing serious), enjoyed getting high with peers while staying in or before going out for the night and was overjoyed with my impressive grades. During this time, I didn't realize how tortured I was—which protected me from my demons doing further damage. I never felt deprived or ravenous while limiting my calorie intake. Remaining in strict control was a new way of numbing my feelings, and avoiding food was a helluva lot easier than fighting to manage it. One of my many life-changing moments occurred the day that my college roommate, Ann, innocently brought up purging. At the time, I wasn't aware that people threw up on purpose. But one day, she randomly asked, "Do you know how to make yourself throw up?" After shaking my head in confusion, she explained, "Put your finger in the back of your throat. My friend told me how to do it, and it works, but I don't like it." I quickly gave it a try by purposely eating more than my usual granola at dinner that night. Just like that, I instantly became bulimic.

When I stopped controlling my life with anorexia, I originally viewed bingeing and purging as literally having my cake and eating it too. It never occurred to me that this was an eating disorder. But in reality, bulimia had me under its spell. My new routine entailed devouring all the food that I'd deprived myself of since the summer before spending twenty torturous minutes leaning over the bowl to bring it back up. After following a restrictive diet for so long, I looked forward to the iffy meals in the school cafeteria. Since certain foods were easier to bring up than others, obsessing about what to eat preoccupied my every thought—even when I was out and about having a good time. I was terrified of being discovered. But after dinner, the girl's public bathroom was usually filled with floormates primping for a night on the town or for a strut on the floor of their current crush. Since they spent more time fussing than going to the bathroom, it was nearly impossible finding moments to purge in secrecy. But I quickly discovered that the shower drowned out my retching. Even better, it had a unique drainage system that is best described as house gutters on the floor that washed away the food to some mystery location. Throwing up eventually became unbearable, but its firm grip didn't allow me to welcome back anorexia or eat like a normal person. Purging after dinner had become as natural as reaching for my toothbrush every morning to eliminate yucky breath. My new routine entailed attending classes during the day before bingeing and purging at night. Despite throwing up, I digested some of the calories and packed on five pounds. Filling out my gaunt frame was a fair price to pay for gorging myself. Plus, my weight didn't make much of a difference since I perceived myself as big with or without the extra pounds.

In addition to my physical transformation, mental illness was at war with my brain. It repeatedly drummed into my head that no one liked me. As a result, I abruptly stopped hanging out with the new friends I'd spent every free minute with at school. Instead, I either studied in my room behind the closed door or used my thirteen-inch black and white Panasonic TV to keep me company. When I heard my friends' laughter drifting from down the hall, I was convinced that they were saying something bad about me. I was living out a self-fulfilling prophecy by existing as the outcast that paranoia accused me of being. But there was no going back because I relied on purging the same way that heroin addicts desperately depend on their fix. Since my mom hadn't seen me since I'd lost and gained back some of the weight, I essentially looked the same to her during Christmas break. That's why a random comment she made after watching a news segment on bulimia blew me away. While describing the bulimic girl she had seen being interviewed on TV, she blurted out of nowhere, "I'll bet you have it too." Without giving it any thought, the words, "I do," flew out of my mouth. She nodded, "I knew it. This bulimia thing has you written all over it." Despite my misguided belief that this was simply a means to maintain a slim figure, my mom booked an appointment with an eating disorder specialist near school. I dismissed everything the therapist said because I was convinced that I was better informed. After three sessions, I left him for good after proclaiming, "Purging isn't a problem, I can stop any time I want." But I discovered how wrong I was when I tried taking a break a few months later and failed miserably.

During sophomore year, my secret was revealed when I bonded with another bulimic girl across the hall. Mandy and I were at the school grocery store to pick up soda when the bright packaging from the cookie aisle caught my eye. I commented, "I swear, I could eat that entire box of Oreos right now." With a sly sideways look, Mandy hinted, "Well, you know you could, right?" Receiving her hidden message loud and clear, I squeezed her arm and squealed, "You too?" Our first binge together included a box of Double Stuff Oreo cookies. After our nightly pig out, we sought relief in the two hall bathrooms. Mandy wasn't as secretive or quiet as I was, and she didn't seem to mind if anyone overheard her retching. Housemates quickly caught on but having a binge partner took away the shame. How bad could it be if Mandy purged too?

When I studied abroad in London for junior year, weak plumbing that wouldn't tolerate undigested food eliminated the option to purge. But I couldn't stop bingeing, and within three months, I packed on about twenty pounds. It didn't help my self-esteem that my roommate had a naturally perfect size two body, without an ounce of fat, that would've made half of Hollywood's actresses jealous as hell. This marked the first time that being overweight wasn't in my head—it was in my puffy face, tight pants and jiggly middle. When I flew home to visit my parents during Easter break, my mom took one look at me and walked away. She didn't need to say a word because her dumbfounded expression said it all, "You can't be happy if you're overweight." That summer, Mandy met me in London to begin a two-month jaunt through Europe. While traveling on a limited budget, we spent most of our money on shopping and very little for food. Between hiking miles every day while sightseeing and not eating much, I easily shed the unwanted pounds. Visiting majestic castles, intriguing ruins and learning about the history of Europe firsthand brought me to a happy place where food didn't haunt my thoughts.

Back in Boston for senior year, I lived alone in an off-campus studio rental. Coming down from the high of Europe and not having friends in the building was a losing combination. The bulimia quickly reappeared and pressured me to make up for lost time. But I could now only successfully purge every other day. This made meal planning a much more time-consuming and arduous task. As bringing up the food became more and more difficult, I looked for other options. Ipecac, an over the counter medicine that causes vomiting, seemed worth a try. But when I violently threw up as if I had a stomach virus, I immediately chucked the rest of the bottle. When a friend invited me to join her and her mom at one of Boston's finest restaurants, I declined with, "I can't go, I already ate lunch and I can't also eat dinner." With a look of bewilderment, she commented, "That's screwed up." Her mother, who is a renowned psychologist, wholeheartedly agreed. My eating ritual became shoving down food every other day without even tasting it and crying afterward with my head in the bowl and fingers down my throat. I desperately needed emotional protection from my demons, so I continued purging for a couple more years. But, eventually, I found the willpower to stop when my hatred for bulimia outweighed my compulsion to push down my feelings with food.

Chapter 5

Devastation, Heartache and First Love

By five o'clock on tequila Fridays at work, the blender was in full mode transforming adults into uninhibited deviants. Joints were passed around at holiday parties as casually as hors d'oeuvres. Everyone was sleeping with each other, especially after tequila Fridays. By the end of the night, wasted people were being shoved into taxis to get home safely or fooling around behind closed office doors. It'll always remain a mystery why Dave's taxi took three hours to get from NYC to Brooklyn—even to Dave! After one Christmas party, I came in to work the next day with beard burn on my face. I couldn't argue with the evidence, so I let the guys bust my chops. Working at an agency that was like Mad Men on steroids gave me a taste of the 60s—my favorite era.

I've always known that my destiny was to be a writer. The orgy-like culture at my first job was an added bonus for a free spirit like me. My talent always played an integral role in my identity and is one of the only qualities that I would never want to change. I wrote poetry in elementary school before tapping into my sordid thoughts to create dark narratives during middle school. When the class was assigned a research paper in high school, everyone moaned and groaned while I secretly couldn't wait to get started. Being a naturally strong writer served me well all throughout my years in school and often made me the teacher's pet. One of my biggest supporters was my dad, who was convinced that I'd inherited my talent from him. But he wanted me to join his law practice. So, every few months, he would have an application from CUNY School of Law mailed to my apartment. I told you he had a great sense of humor. He didn't stop until I won my first advertising award in my mid-twenties and proudly placed it on my parent's mantle. If I was happy, he was happy.

Journalism was my major in college, but from the get-go, I knew that it wasn't for me. Reading articles in class from reporters who had the gall to ask questions like, "How do you feel now that your twenty-year-old son has been killed by a gang member?" made me cringe. There was no way in hell that I could ask such sensitive questions while maintaining my composure. Plus, I had less than zero desire to do so. But I still knew in my heart that I was a writer for life. My mom wisely advised, "Get an internship in a different area of writing and see if you like it." Advertising seemed cool, and after actually listening to her for once, I was hired as an intern at a two-person agency conveniently located across the street from school. Writing my very first pun became my aha moment when I knew exactly where my career was headed. I'd made up a dental chew product for humans, and the ad I wrote depicted a few people sitting around the table at a restaurant while the headline read: *Cleans teeth in those hard to clean places*. My internship mentor was impressed with my quick wit and encouraged me to pursue advertising. Since I fell in love with copywriting during my senior year of college, I needed to put together a portfolio of writing samples before applying for jobs. But I was a type-A personality to the core and anxious to enter the working world. My mom kept repeating, "Start as a secretary and work your way up." I responded with conviction, "If I have to work as a secretary, it has to be in the creative department at an advertising agency." When I accepted a secretarial role right before graduation, it was sheer luck that I landed a job at one of the top agencies in NYC. I envisioned getting promoted by proving my worth. During the day I was, "Please make a copy, Sharon." In night class, I morphed into the determined "I-won't-be-a-secretary-for-long-copywriter-in-training."

Being a feisty baby-faced twenty-two-year-old, I received my fair share of male attention and got away with a snarky attitude because the men thought I was cute. Sexist or not, that was the culture in advertising back then. But the women in HR wanted to throw me in the Hudson River wearing cement boots, and I don't blame them. I'd suddenly become the depraved kid who was always called to the principal's office. When one of the top creatives asked me to fill out purchase orders, "I don't do purchase orders," was my pithy response. It became an office joke, but the manager who got stuck doing them wasn't amused. Silence has always made me crawl out of my skin, which often led to my saying the one thing that was better left unsaid. It's a bit like turrets because no matter how hard I tried sitting quietly, the words spilled out of my mouth. But bringing attention to myself also served me well by making my career aspirations known and engaging my boss, Joe, to mentor me. He suggested, "You should take writing courses at the School of Visual Arts. Show me the class list, and I'll tell you who the best teachers are." Heeding his advice, I honed my craft at night school while simultaneously putting together a portfolio. Every Monday before class, Joe critiqued my work and encouraged me with positive reinforcement when he wasn't sending me back with, "Give it another shot." He felt that I had potential and began trusting me with small agency assignments that no one else could be bothered with.

For my first account, I created a weekly radio spot for Six Flags Great Adventure with bigger-than-life personalities like Jay Thomas. Owning an account was a rare responsibility for a junior writer. It didn't get any better than being paid to have fun while learning from some of the best creatives in the business. This became one of the luckiest breaks in my career. Despite negative Sharon always giving herself a bad rap, not everything in life was shit. The fact is that some of it was pretty damn good. Becoming one of the only female creatives to successfully break into advertising in the 1980s was what kept me sane during those times when everything else around me was falling apart. My routine as a secretary entailed arriving before 9 a.m. and immediately calling my father after grabbing a cup of tea with milk. My greeting to him when he answered my call was always "What." Even if I didn't feel like talking, I felt compelled to call him to tell him that I didn't feel like talking.

After proving my writing chops, I was promoted within five months to the role of junior copywriter at the prestigious Della Femina & Travisano agency. On my first official day as a creative, my dad sent me an assortment of red and yellow tulips in a tall, etched crystal vase. Sticking out between the colorful flower petals was a white card in his distinctive chicken scratch that read, "To a copywriter extraordinaire." This simple business-sized card will always be my most prized possession. The first time that she heard my amusing radio spot for Finlandia cheese, my mom called crying. My parents were my biggest cheerleaders and added tremendous joy to my budding career.

The creative department shared an unfiltered camaraderie where everyone said whatever was on their mind, and the only PC was the world's first computers. Being told things like, "Your chest looks good in that shirt, you should wear it more often," was taken as a compliment. Since the men were a good-looking and stylish bunch, I respected their opinions.

Mike was a sweet copywriter who sucked at hiding his schoolboy crush on me. So, when he complimented me right after I gave purging a rest, it was all the impetus I needed to stop. The beginning of the end began when my coworker Shelly and I made plans to stay at her mom's house in Hawaii. There was no way that I was going to taint her home by throwing up, so my eating disorder took a vacation too. I was an average weight, but unbeknownst to me, the bile that came up with my food had puffed up my cheeks. The swelling in my face must've gone down because upon my return to work, Mike commented, "You look so thin, Sharon. Did you lose a shitload of weight?" Being 100 percent sure that I was the same size, I concluded that my face must've looked thinner. I didn't realize that bulimia gave me chipmunk cheeks. But thanks to my coworker and vanity, the bingeing stopped pretty much on the spot—except for a few weak moments during the holidays. Thanksgiving was my favorite day and always my greatest challenge. Never did I think it would be so easy to stop, but once my mind was made up, it didn't take much effort.

While I was producing notable work, trouble brewed when a new creative director was brought in after an agency merger. I tried staying out of his way, but my big mouth and sassy attitude drew unwanted attention. Things got worse when I had words with his *not-so-secret* girlfriend at the agency with whom he was having an affair. A month after his arrival, he called me into his expansive corner office that faced ritzy Madison Avenue. He said something along the lines of, "It's probably better if you find somewhere else to work," before firing me on the spot with, "You can pack up your things and leave. Today is your last day." I was devastated as my demons taunted me that I could add never finding another job to my fear of dying alone.

My one-person pity party was interrupted when Alyce called because my parents wanted to say goodbye before setting off on their long-anticipated trip to Paris. I tried really hard to hide the fact that I'd gotten the ax, but each sob and sniffle gave me away. When she asked what was wrong, I could hear my mom in the background questioning, "Why is Sharon crying?" Worried that I might do something extreme, my parents immediately canceled their trip. Her intuition knew that I wasn't going to just be OK and search for another job. She'd seen me fall before, and she was the only one who knew how to soften the landing. In an attempt to cheer me up and still get away for a few days, my mom booked the three of us a trip to Montreal. Through no fault of her own, it turned out not to be one of her brightest ideas. I sobbed during the entire eight hour drive and challenged my dad's unlimited patience. My parents tried consoling me all throughout the trip, with my dad cracking his usual jokes. But this time, I didn't find anything that he said amusing. He finally lost it and yelled at me to stop crying, which only elevated my sniffling to bawling. Trying to cheer me up was futile. Depression swooped in the second that I was fired and held a tight grip until a new job temporarily kicked my demons back to the curb. For me, depression didn't appear out of nowhere. All my episodes were triggered by a catastrophic event. But I thought that suffering prolonged sadness was the norm, especially since I had nothing to compare it to. Only later did I learn that crying for months on end or shedding ten pounds in a weekend wasn't normal. It's called clinical depression.

Club Med

Within two months of losing my job, I was offered a new one at another prominent advertising agency. "Junior" was dropped from my title, and my salary was inflated by a whopping twelve thousand dollars. My college friend Ellen was free to spontaneously travel with me right before I was going to begin my new job after the new year.

We settled on Turks & Caicos Club Med, one of the newer resorts at the time that catered to young singles like ourselves. Ellen and I flew together, and upon arrival, she made a beeline to the pool while I took my sweet time unpacking. I later found her flirting with two hunks who appeared to be around our age. They politely held out their hands while introducing themselves as Danny and Steven. Steven immediately grabbed my attention with his black wavy hair, cute oversized ears and adorable Midwestern accent. His undeniable sense of humor solidified my instantaneous crush. I don't remember what he joked about at the pool, but after spilling milk later in the day, he pointed at it and remarked, "Don't cry." Most people wouldn't immediately get the joke, let alone quickly think of something that witty to say. My trip had unexpectedly turned into the beginning of young love, and everything finally seemed to be falling into place. Perhaps I wasn't going to die alone after all.

Initially, we juggled a long-distance relationship. Since Steven wasn't earning a salary as a medical resident in Chicago, I paid to fly out from New York and visit him once or twice a month. It felt like all was right in the world as we acted like two teenagers in the throes of young love. Some of my favorite memories include falling in love with Chicago's deep dish pizza after tasting it for the first time and zooming down beautiful Lakefront Drive, where Steven pointed out where Oprah lived. Right before the summer, Steven arranged to do part of his residency in Manhattan. I'd never shared my home with a man before, but my parents didn't question my living with a nice Jewish doctor. (A few months later, I learned why they seemed so desperate for me to marry Steven ASAP.) I was the happiest that I'd ever been and envisioned spending the rest of my life with this man, who wooed me with his endearing poems, goofy cards and three-page letters.

But he also seemed too good to be true. When Steven's personality did a 180 toward the end of the summer, I suspected him of cheating. The dead giveaway was when he bluntly came out and asked, "What does it mean if a girl wears a wedding ring on a chain around her neck? Is she married?" After questioning him nonstop about why he was acting so cold, he viciously spewed, "I don't love you anymore. I don't think I ever loved you." Those two sentences broke my heart, shattered my dreams and crushed all hope of my not dying alone. But I didn't try to talk Steven out of leaving because I've always believed that you can't force someone to love you. He moved out the next day while I remained curled up in the fetal position for the entire weekend and lost ten pounds.

Having somebody who seemed so perfect slip through my fingers didn't surprise me. My happily-ever-after died many years ago on the day of the abortion. It took me years to realize that by cheating on me, Steven was far less amazing than I'd given him credit for. The following Monday, my coworkers couldn't stop staring at me upon observing my obvious weight loss. My boss offered, "Let me take you out to lunch. You need to be fed." Subtlety was never his strong suit. This was the second depression that sucked the life out of me for several months. Simple things like seeing couples holding hands at the corner grocery store instantly put a lump in my throat. While I contemplated suicide, I never came close to finding the nerve to follow through. The sadness eventually lessened with time, and a year later, I was over mourning a cheater. But the fear of remaining single and dying alone was gathering strength by the day. When my nasty demons whispered that I'd never find someone else to love me, I knew they were right.

Bad News

Soon after my breakup with Steven, my parents sat me and my sister down to deliver shockingly upsetting news. The next two minutes would change my life forever.

They'd known for a while that my dad was suffering from a rare blood cancer. Even worse, there was no cure. In my mind, everything negative was punishment for the abortion, and nothing could be worse than my beloved daddy leaving me so young. He was diagnosed at fifty-six with myelofibrosis when a routine checkup detected slight anemia. After running more tests, the doctor broke the news, "You have an incurable illness, and most of my patients don't survive ten years post-diagnosis." The bone marrow breaks down in people who suffer from this rare blood disease, which means that they can no longer make the red blood cells needed to carry oxygen throughout their body. Blood transfusions buy the sufferer time, but eventually, the body suffers from too much spleen and liver damage and dies. When his blood count level first reached borderline low, my dad's only symptom was fatigue. To protect me and my sister, my parents hid his illness until it progressed to the point of requiring blood transfusions. All I can remember hearing is deep, loud snores emanating from the partially closed bedroom door. If he began napping for a longer amount of time, or more frequently, Alyce and I never noticed.

The weekend before his initial transfusion, my mom gathered us into the den to have her long-dreaded conversation. I'll bet she'd already rehearsed it in her head hundreds of times. My dad sat silently on the arm of the infamous puffy red couch, avoiding eye contact by inspecting his short fingernails. My mom said something along the lines of, "Daddy has a cancer of the bone. He's going to start receiving blood transfusions to give him energy and make him feel better." I jumped up to hug and squeeze him while pleading, "You're not going to die, are you?" I'll never forget his response: "We all die at some point, but hopefully, not soon." It took my mom a couple of minutes to explain my dad's incurable disease and a year for it to sink in. To protect myself, I put his mortality out of my mind until emergency hospital visits smashed reality in my face.

Similar to having your life flash before your eyes, all the future events that my dad might miss out on played in my head like a film on fast forward. Who was going to walk me down the aisle if I found someone to marry, and would my future children ever experience the yucky wet kisses on the nose that their Poppy loved to give? Ironically, before I learned that he was sick, I often hugged him tightly and declared, "I love you so much, you can never die." There's no doubt how unintentionally guilty my declaration of love must've made my dad feel. His response was always, "I'm not going anywhere," and I imagine he silently added a "yet" at the end of his sentence. I'm grateful that my parents initially hid his illness. This gave me more time to enjoy a normal relationship. Otherwise, I'm sure I would've obsessed about his illness and ruined the time that we had left together. As my dad grew weaker, Alyce and I were overly protective of him. But it wasn't until he could barely remain upright on his own that he put aside his pride and accepted the help that we continually offered. The dirty stares that healthy-looking Dad received when parking in handicapped spots became looks of pity when he resembled a walking zombie. It was so much easier feeling the anger of judgment than the pity of strangers. Since I learned about his illness a few months after crashing from the breakup with Steven, being on a slow trajectory back up helped me deal with the situation better. I probably would've sunk into a profound depression if I'd received the news while everything else in my life was going well.

Maybe I Won't Die Alone

After sorting through fifty Polaroids, I chose two men. One I'd never meet, and the other I married exactly a year later.

A few months after learning about my dad's illness, I met Ed through a 1990s version of online dating. Members traveled to *People Resource's* fifty-seventh street office to sort through Polaroids, pop in a VHS of those who piqued their interest and send an invitation if they wanted to meet. If the person liked them back, they were handed a piece of paper with the other person's phone number. Ed was smart, intellectual, well-traveled and kind, the type of man I envisioned marrying. He was also Jewish—which meant a lot to me and everything to my somewhat religious father. Our little inside joke was that Ed paid two thousand dollars for me while I spent fourteen hundred on him. He signed up because traveling half the year for his bank job made dating difficult. I joined to avoid remaining single and dying alone. My strong opinionated personality complimented Ed's reserved, calm demeanor, and we immediately meshed as a couple. Twenty-three years later, what stands out the most about Ed's tape was his bragging about his mango chutney dip. He was right; it was pretty damn good. From our first date feasting on dim sum in Chinatown, I knew that Ed was the one. On the other hand, he teased me that he wasn't sure about marrying me until his proposal a few months later. Two weeks after our first date, we began spending every night together and quickly became a couple. My fondest memory from early on in our relationship happened when Ed made me tuna fish for the first time. When I complained, "It tastes different, I don't like it," Ed responded, "It's not the canned crap, I made it from fresh tuna." That's when I declared, "I don't want fresh tuna, it's disgusting. I can only eat tuna from a can." So much for Ed's exceptional cooking skills.

A month into our relationship, we booked a trip to California's Napa Valley. Even though I don't drink, I was looking forward to touring the picturesque vineyards while being the designated driver so that Ed could enjoy a good buzz. But my dad insisted on first meeting the man who was taking away his twenty-eight-year-old baby girl. I considered his old fashioned mindset adorable and gladly respected his wishes. Ed casually replied with his easygoing attitude, "Sure, should we go on Saturday or Sunday?" On the way to my parents, I kept my nervous energy at bay by constantly switching songs on the radio like a DJ at a bar mitzvah. Ed and I were only together for a month, but I knew that this was the beginning of our future as husband and wife. There was never a doubt in my mind that both parents would instantly take to him, and I was right. I savored every precious moment as we gathered around the kitchen table for lunch and conversation. My whole body smiled while seeing my dad animated for the first time in months. While my mom tried playing it cool, the pep in her step gave her away. The conversation naturally flowed as if Ed had always been a part of the family. I could detect a subtle smirk on my dad's face as we described our plans. Engrossed in conversation, he didn't take a nap until after we left. That's when I knew that he approved of and trusted Ed to take care of me. To top it off, my in-laws and parents became fast friends upon meeting a month later.

On our first date, I explained my dad's illness to Ed so that he understood why my running to the hospital at a moment's notice had become standard procedure. He didn't flinch when I told him or complain when he had to drop everything to drive me to the hospital. It was both poor and perfect timing that I met him three years before my dad died. When I started bringing up marriage about four months into our relationship, Ed always described us as "Being on the same trajectory." Seven months after our first date, my apartment lease was about to expire, but I wouldn't move in with Ed until he put a ring on my finger. More importantly, the clock was ticking. Delaying the engagement increased the odds that my dad wouldn't be alive to walk me down the aisle. A month later, we were at my jeweler selecting a beautiful round colorless diamond that wasn't too small for my high standards, nor too big for Ed's conservative taste.

We officially became engaged on August 7, 1992. While it was a memorable proposal, it didn't sweep me off my feet. My dream proposal included the man getting down on one knee while going on and on about how much he adored me and couldn't live without me. But after

Ed picked up the ring, he handed me yellow stickies with clues written on where to find it. Couch pillows flew as I scavenged the apartment. The last clue sent me straight to his front suit pocket. After practically pushing him over, I plucked out my beautiful ring and put it on my ever-so-ready finger. Ed said, "OK, I'm hungry, let's eat. You in the mood for pizza?" I guess I'll never hear those magic words, "Will you marry me?"

A Wedding to Remember

After calling my mom with the expected but nonetheless exciting news, she began running around like the stereotypical manic wedding planner you see in the movies. Putting together an elegant wedding was in her element. Plus, it gave her a much-needed distraction from my dad's illness.

It was crucial that we select a date quickly on such short notice and start searching for a venue immediately. Many places were available the day after Christmas, but Ed nixed the idea of sharing his birthday with our anniversary. I then chose January ninth, exactly one year since we'd met and not a popular wedding season, given New York's unpredictable winter weather. While taking my dad's napping needs into consideration, we selected the Plaza Hotel's Ambassador room. It was a beautiful fairytale setting overlooking the greenery on the southern edge of Central Park and available on such short notice. The whirlwind called Mom held me captive as we drove around New York to book a photographer and band, order a cake from the famous Sylvia Weinstock and pick out the invitations, color theme and menu.

After that, it was straight to Kleinfeld's to fulfill every little girl's dream of trying on wedding dresses. My mom was speechless as I twirled around the store, modeling the second of eight possible options. Despite the fact that many women search for months, I said yes to the dress within an hour. Through happy tears, my mom exclaimed, "That's the dress. I knew it the second you walked out of the dressing room." I called my dad to describe the magnificent ballgown that my mom and I immediately fell in love with. Its breathtaking elegance ensured that

I'd be the center of attention. For once in my life, I wanted all eyes on me because I knew that I was never going to look or feel this beautiful again. The gown was tastefully sexy with a formfitting bodice, buttons straight up the back and sheer lace on the arms and upper chest. From the waist down, there were multiple layers of flowing tulle that made me feel like a princess ballerina. My dad's response was exactly what I expected, "I can't wait to see it, my little girl is going to look beautiful." After selecting the dress and getting measured for alterations, my mom continued frantically running around to ensure that the day would be perfect. It felt like a blessing giving the entire family something happy to look forward to and providing my dad with a tangible reason to keep fighting to stay alive.

When the most important day of my life finally arrived, all eyes were transfixed on me as my parents and I slowly descended the deep red-carpeted aisle. Halfway down, kisses were planted simultaneously on both sides of my cheeks before I glided the rest of the way alone—I was headed into Ed's outstretched arms. Happy tears sat like puddles that threatened to ruin an hour's worth of professional makeup. Dreams did come true, and best of all, my dad was alive and wore a permanent grin throughout the evening. He was already seriously ill, but an outsider never would've suspected that in a few weeks, his six-pound spleen was going to be removed. As word spread about his pending surgery, more than one person remarked, "You can't be that sick, Murray. You look great." He considered my wedding his last hurrah given the slim-to-none chance that he'd be alive to meet his first grandchild. I've only been able to watch the wedding video once since he died. It's both sad and surreal seeing him alive and planting kisses on my nose every chance he could steal. Since his passing, I've often wondered something. Is it better to suffer a slow death but have the chance to say goodbye or die instantly? In my dad's case, I'm beyond grateful that he survived for nine years after his diagnosis. But when I go, I pray it's in a flash with zero suffering involved. Dying in my sleep would be nice.

Sharon Greenwald

Two days after the wedding, Ed and I hopped on a grueling twenty-one-hour flight to Singapore. We were headed on a three-week, four-countries honeymoon. The sweet stewardess surprised us with a bucket of champagne after we mentioned being newlyweds. Since business class was unusually empty, Ed stretched out across our two oversized seats for most of the flight. After unsuccessfully fighting to sleep in the row behind him, I passed the time by polishing off two James Patterson novels. Being married both did and didn't make me feel different. We were still the same two people who loved each other. But it felt more special and secure since we'd taken our vows. It was damn good knowing that I married a wonderful man and wouldn't die alone. Marriage was as amazing as I always imagined, and I had no doubt in the world that it'd last forever. Until it didn't.

All throughout his career, Ed changed time zones a zillion times for work. So, he knew I'd acclimate to Singapore time easier by staying up until at least seven o'clock local time. But after our first meal in Asia, and much negotiation, I was fast asleep by six o'clock. Ed gave in to me most of the time and carefully picked his battles. This made it easy for me to know when I'd crossed the line and needed to back off. Several years into our marriage when Ed really pissed me off, I purposely kept goading him until he lost it. We were polar opposites but surprisingly compatible about practically everything. Both of us were morning people, preferred active vacations over vegetating on the beach and shared the same Asian style of decoration. But there was one exception that eventually doomed our marriage—chemistry. Our two vastly different personalities carried over to the bedroom, and I realized that our relationship would be based more on friendship than romance. No two people are exactly alike, so I thought that my being more sexual was a compromise that I'd have to make. But now that Ed was the only man who I'd be intimate with for the rest of my life, compromise eventually led to frustration. In dreams, my subconscious warned me that this was an issue. But my brain refused to process the information until all hell broke loose in the summer of 2005.

Chapter 6

Pregnancy, Motherhood and Mental Illness

"How much time does he have?" I asked. The doctor fixed his eyes on my dad and said, "Ask Murray, he should already be dead." Nothing was going to stop him from meeting the next generation of Applemans. For once, his stubbornness came in handy.

Ed was a successful banker who provided the good life, which supported our fondness for immediate gratification. It wasn't uncommon to glimpse a pricey antique, purchase it on the spur of the moment and later find a place for it in the house. Getting married at the ages of twenty-nine and thirty-three, our impatience extended to becoming parents. I desperately wanted my dad alive to meet the first grandchild on both sides of the family. Ed envisioned being a relatively young dad. We were in total agreement and ecstatic when a pregnancy test revealed a double line four months after the wedding. But one day at work around my sixth week of pregnancy, I went from bliss to panic. As I was using the bathroom, I freaked out upon discovering that bright red blood had stained my panties and gone through the crotch of my jeans. Ed was his usual calm self when I met him at the doctor's office thirty minutes later. The technician drew blood to check my hormone levels while the doctor assured us that most women who spot during pregnancy go on to have healthy babies. Ed accepted this comment as fact, meaning that there was nothing to worry about. But my negative mind knew that this pregnancy wasn't going to end on a positive note.

Ed often dismissed my concerns and, instead, would accuse me of overreacting. It was frustrating because most of the time, my response was legitimate and appropriate. But having an animated delivery and being as emotional as Ed was stoic, he didn't take my excitability seriously. There was a real chance I was having a miscarriage, which meant losing precious time before my dad lost his fight with death. It was now a waiting game to see if the bleeding would stop. That weekend, Ed had plans to go camping with friends while I'd stay home. I didn't dare express my fear of being alone if I miscarried because that would be akin to asking for help. If he adored me, he never would've considered leaving me when I needed his love and support. I shouldn't have to ask. Ed only bowed out of the trip when one of his camping buddy's wives called and scolded, "Under no circumstance are you to leave Sharon alone." The fact that he'd even considered leaving me during such a vulnerable time was a huge disappointment.

I was still bleeding after the weekend, so back to the doctor's office we went. The situation was no longer taken lightly when the doctor saw me and exclaimed, "You're still bleeding? I thought it would stop by now." It was oddly validating that I wasn't overreacting as the doctor and Ed had subtly implied. Blood tests confirmed that my HCG levels weren't doubling as they would in a healthy pregnancy. During the ultrasound, I noticed the technician scrunch her forehead and stare a bit too long at the screen. Hesitantly, she remarked, "I see two sacks." I was miscarrying at seven weeks with what turned out to be twins. The pain was doubled when the doctor came in to quietly console me, "I'm so sorry, the pregnancy isn't viable." Miscarrying was punishment for the abortion that I had thirteen years earlier, and no one could've convinced me otherwise. When the bleeding didn't stop, I was forced to have a D&C—which is essentially the same procedure as an abortion. As we approached the clinic the following day, Ed and I encountered a few pro-life protestors outside with their white signs reading *Abortion*

Kills held high. Despite already feeling guilty as hell, I tried to defend myself. "I want these babies, I don't have a choice," were the last words that I uttered before walking in to face my punishment. Years later, my mom recalled that when she told my dad the news, "He lost all hope and cried." I can imagine him holding his hands over his face while tears fell through his long fingers. It was a race against time, and his emotional pain was harder to bear than the loss of my unborn babies.

After becoming pregnant again on the first try, both families acted as if I was carrying the Messiah. Get-togethers now entailed everyone rubbing my belly while talking to the fast-growing bump we'd already named Morgan. My mind silently pleaded with my dad's body to keep fighting. Three weeks into my pregnancy, the smell of everything from chicken to Chinese food sent me racing to the bathroom. This intense, around-the-clock nausea took off ten pounds. While the eating disorder inside of me was thrilled with losing weight, the doctor warned, "You're pregnant, you're not supposed to lose weight. And you have large ketones. If you don't start eating, I'm admitting you to the hospital!" Eating a Carvel ice cream cone with sprinkles every night during the coldest winter on record did the trick. Despite nonstop suffering, the constant nausea served its purpose by reassuring my paranoia that the baby was okay.

Right before giving birth, I was traumatized by an experience on one of my last commutes home. It was a record-breaking, oppressive humid day in August when the only people not complaining about the heat were those indoors with air conditioning. While approaching the 5:29 express from the steamy platform, I couldn't understand why half of the cars were empty. Curious, I had to check things out for myself. Before walking in, I was overpowered with a heat similar to an oven that has been baking for an hour at 400 degrees. I quickly discovered that a lack of air conditioning was the culprit. There was no way in hell that I could sit in the stifling heat without passing out. But as I inched my way forward into the packed air-conditioned car with Morgan in my belly leading the way, I couldn't find an empty seat. This was a situation when not feeling worthy of asking for help put me in a bind. I couldn't possibly stand for half an hour, but I felt guilty taking someone else's seat. They didn't want to stand either. As I stood looking like a vertical beached whale, the passengers closest to me buried their heads in their newspapers. Their futile attempt to make me vanish was clearly evident. I internally panicked while fighting to hold back tears. Thankfully, a man looked up and asked if I wanted his seat. Too choked up for words, I simply nodded. I'm pretty sure that the girl behind me, who was not-so-silently cursing everyone out for making a very pregnant woman stand, shared my relief.

On my due date, "Go to work, I'm not having the baby this week," was my response to Ed wondering if he should stay home. After explaining my rationale, he kissed me and my belly goodbye before bolting out the door in an attempt to catch his regular 6:32 train. Despite my due date falling on August 18, both Ed's and my first cousin were born on August 25. I instinctively knew that the universe had the same plan for Morgan. On the morning of August 24, I rolled over after being startled awake by Ed's alarm and felt my first contraction. "You're not going to work today," was all I needed to say. Later in the day, Ed wouldn't get off a conference call until I threatened to leave without him when his "One more minute" became an hour.

By four o'clock that afternoon, I was updating my dad and Alyce during the forty-minute drive from Westchester into Manhattan. The conversation was interrupted every three minutes when a contraction rendered me speechless. Ed remained calm while I sat backward in the front seat, grunting and grimacing through every excruciating squeeze. Tired of being as big as a house and unable to remember what my feet looked like, I tolerated the intense agony that my mom called *happy pain*. Let's face it, it's not like I had a choice. But my obstetrician wrongly assumed that a first-time mother would progress slowly. So, she took her time getting to the hospital. The entire maternity ward heard me freaking out as I labored naturally for eight and a half centimeters. "I want drugs! The doctor promised me drugs!" resonated from one end of the long maternity ward to the other. When Dr. Livoti finally arrived and gave the go-ahead, the anesthesiologist administered an epidural. Once he was done, I professed my undying love. It's a fact that the maternity ward is at its fullest during a full moon. My spirited Morgan was appropriately born during, you guessed it, a full moon. It was so crowded that I didn't have a room until right before it was time to push.

If I was watching my loved one in so much pain and had zero control over the situation, I'd probably pass out. But Ed didn't flinch. After trying to push out what felt like an overinflated basketball for forty minutes, he glanced down and amusingly exclaimed, "There's hair between your legs." At 12:37 a.m. on August 25, Morgan Elisabeth Greenwald made her grand entrance into the world with a full head of sticky black hair. She announced her arrival from full juicy lips that adorably quivered with every piercing scream.

Five fingers, five toes, a full head of hair and great lips. You'd think that I was on my way to the imagined *happily ever after*. But I was envious of Ed's obvious joy at the sight of our loud, beautiful baby while I internally panicked. Despite everything, meeting and holding Morgan for the first time will always be one of my most miraculous moments. Now that the physical pain of labor was gone, I was beyond relieved. But the sadness and emotional pain that swooped in to take its place felt equally overwhelming. The second that Morgan popped out I felt an indescribable emptiness that I'd never experienced before. The world had lost its color as everything turned black and blurry. I was oblivious as to what this feeling was and how to deal with it. It would've helped immensely if postpartum depression was covered in my *What to Expect When You're Expecting* book. But the author didn't add that part in until after Brook Shield's brought postpartum out of the closet. They say that a baby changes everything. And while my love for Morgan took my breath away, postpartum depression stole the joy of becoming a first-time mother. It's a loss that haunts me to this day, especially when I see women happily fussing over their tiny newborn, enjoying every burp, poo and coo.

Having zero experience taking care of a baby, my challenging pregnancy extended into motherhood. Terror struck as I quickly realized that the fantasy of becoming a parent was far different than the harsh reality. During Morgan's first diaper change, I was petrified of accidentally ripping off her tiny chicken leg. I passed her to Ed and said, "You do it." Fortunately, Ed was the most wonderful hands-on dad and did a great job, so all of Morgan's body parts remained intact. She was colicky from hour one, and her well-developed vocal cords amazed the staff and hospital visitors alike. Ed and I later discovered that most newborns cried at half of her decibel level. That explained why she received a 10/10 on her Apgar test—the first perfect score that the doctor had ever given throughout her long career.

The high point of my pregnancy was that my dad hung on, despite scaring us with a few emergency hospital visits. Alyce described him as practically running from the parking garage to the hospital even though he no longer had the energy to walk two feet to the bathroom. When they entered my hospital room, I asked, "Have you already seen the baby?" I'll never forget my dad's beautiful reply, "You're my baby, and I had to see you first." My mom's annual spa retreat with friends was always booked for the last week of August. When I practically begged her to switch weeks, she said, "I want to go with my friends. This is the one week of the year that I can focus on myself." At the time, I felt abandoned and unloved. But as I later learned more about her isolation while taking care of my dad, I've wholeheartedly forgiven her.

When they wheeled Morgan to my room every two hours for a feeding, she announced her pending arrival from down the hall. My little girl was ready to go. But I wasn't emotionally ready to take care of a cactus, let alone a fussy baby. Within five hours of giving birth, I encountered one of the greatest challenges of motherhood. After the nurse dropped off Morgan in her little plastic incubator, she left me alone to figure out breastfeeding. But feedings in the hospital consisted of me and Morgan staring into each other's almond-shaped eyes and wondering, "Who are you?" I'd made the mistake of checking off the breastfeeding box on my admittance form. But my chest didn't hurt or leak like the *What to Expect When You're Expecting* book described. This was a telltale sign that I wasn't producing milk. Despite the fact that it was my body, the La Leche people refused to let me bottle feed. They reasoned, "It takes time. Just let the baby suck and colostrum will come out." I wouldn't have acquiesced if my hospital stay was longer, or my emotional state was stronger. I'm not sure how my mom failed to warn me that the milk-producing gene is missing in our family. Not having the option to breastfeed relieved a lot of guilt since I didn't have a choice. My body wasn't cooperating, and there wasn't a thing I could do about it.

The hospital kicked me out less than twenty-four hours later. On the way to the car, Ed asked, "Why are you waddling like a duck?" He also didn't understand why I was sitting lopsided on my left butt cheek when we began our drive home. My answer to everything became, "I have a hemorrhoid the size of Gibraltar, and it hurts like hell." Ed thought that I was exaggerating until he looked between my legs and nearly passed out. He described my hemorrhoid as looking like a big mushroom attached to my butt. I didn't dare inspect it for myself because I knew that it was something that I could never unsee. After that, Ed was a lot more understanding whenever I whined about my excruciating painful tushy.

During Morgan's very first bottle feeding at home, she scoffed down a whopping three ounces. Babies supposedly don't need to drink for the first couple of days. But Morgan sucked the nipple so hard that it took all my strength to pull it out for a burp. In my mind, starving her was proof of my already being a failure as a mother. We hired a baby nurse predominantly for night feedings. But within hours, there was a change of plans. Upon hearing Morgan's first tiny squeak, I made my way to heat a bottle in the kitchen like Pavlov's dog. Despite suffering postpartum depression, my powerful mother's intuition always kept me ahead of her needs. I enjoyed feedings in the wee hours of the morning when it was so quiet you could hear the silence. My nose explored Morgan's intoxicating scent as I gently rocked and fed her. Even today, the smell of baby lotion boosts my endorphins. Ed often commented, "Wow, Morgan slept through the night," to which I'd reply with a bit of sarcasm, "No, you slept through the night. I was up with her four times."

On the second day home from the hospital, Morgan was on display in the living room as she napped in her white straw-like bassinet. She was intermittently taking sucks in her sleep from her pacifier, which we discovered early on was the answer to preserving our hearing. All four grandparents stared at the baby, who was anointed *the most beautiful grandchild in the entire world*. Every time someone stood over the bassinet, they'd report back on who Morgan looked like. Apparently, she resembled at least six relatives from both sides of the family. My dad sat at the end of the couch wearing his familiar grin, probably thinking what no one dared to speak out loud. In addition to Morgan's birth, he was celebrating the fact that he was alive to meet her. Ed stayed home from work the first week to spend precious time with our newborn while I struggled to decompress both physically and emotionally. My hormones were hopping up and down like jumping beans, my butt had grown a mushroom and my flabby body reminded me of a formerly obese person who desperately needs skin removal surgery.

Depression turned normal new mother challenges into catastrophic events. Since babies don't come with instructions, we spent the first week trying to figure out our fussy crybaby. Feedings initially consisted of spit up that stained the couch and soiled the shirt of whichever unfortunate person was feeding her. Ed once came dashing into the kitchen with his shirt full of something that looked like feta cheese. When I asked, "What the hell is on your shirt?" he replied, "It's Morgan's formula. She literally blew chunks." As I spoke to the pediatrician while crying hysterically, I could detect a slight *I'm used to getting calls like this from first-time mothers* chuckle in his voice. Dr. Berman suggested, "Why don't you put her on soy, and we'll see how she tolerates it." That was the third formula we'd try before discovering that soy milk was the answer to more uneventful feedings and fewer stained shirts. But we could still set our clocks to Morgan screeching like a cat in heat between her evening witching hours of five and nine o'clock. Unlike every other single baby in the world, car rides didn't rock her to sleep. None of this phased Ed. Their instant bonding made me feel worse, which I didn't think at the time was possible.

I wasn't sure how to feel after pushing out a seven-pound human being. But I knew that something was out of whack when my nerves were constantly on edge, and happy moments were hard to find. At my two-week checkup, the obstetrician asked how I was feeling. When I answered, "I don't know, kind of down," she didn't delve any further. Instead, she brushed it away with, "Oh, that's normal, everyone gets blue." If it was today, I'm pretty sure that the doctor would've sent me straight to a psychiatrist after I shared regretting being a mother. Looking back, I had no clue how depression was putting distance between my bonding with Morgan and my marriage with Ed. But I'd find out soon enough. When my mom observed me struggling, she offered to bring back the baby nurse. Feeling physically better without a mushroom on my butt this time around made it a far better experience. Full-time help provided the freedom that I so desperately pined for.

As soon as the nurse returned, I updated her on Morgan's needs and feeding schedule before sprinting out the door to run errands. Accomplishing simple tasks like buying toothpaste without a ten-minute struggle with the baby car seat was a refreshing change. The walls of the house were closing in, and something mundane like running errands alone helped me keep my shit together. I couldn't take back being a mother, so I was forced to deal with it—while keeping most of my inner turmoil to myself. Ed and the family knew that something was off, but they had no idea how broken I was inside. It didn't help matters that Morgan was colicky and gave her lungs a workout whether she was cuddled in my arms or swaddled in the crib.

Every morning, I'd safely place her in bed before drowning out the screeching with a hot cascading shower. I looked forward to those five relaxing minutes with the same anticipation once saved for weekends. Upon picking up Morgan after my shower, exhaustion from bawling her eyes out often led to her curling up in my arms for a five-minute catnap. Sweet moments, like feeling my baby's warm breath against my neck, provided revitalization for the next mommy challenge. But everything I did well couldn't erase the infinite times that I berated myself for not being a perfect mother. Today, I completely empathize when I hear about a postpartum woman going batshit crazy.

On the third day home, my dad requested that we bring Morgan to temple for a baby naming. My automatic response was, "No, it's still difficult to walk and painful to sit." But after much coaxing from my mom and giving it a second thought, Ed and I knew that we couldn't, and wouldn't, refuse him this one last gift. The ceremony took place when Morgan was five days old, and the memory of the entire family beaming in temple will forever be seared in my heart. My biggest fear was that colicky Morgan would disrupt the service by screaming to the high heavens—which I guess might've been appropriate in temple. But she slept the entire time while sucking on her beloved pacifier like Maggie from the Simpsons. She was a chip off the old block, and temple put her to sleep in the same way that it bored me. A small Russian bar mitzvah also took place that day. There were only a handful of guests, so the service had an intimacy like nothing I'd ever experienced in temple before. The juxtaposition of celebrating a new life and a thirteen-year-old boy becoming a man was beautiful. After the bar mitzvah boy read from the Torah, I carried Morgan onto the pulpit for the rabbi's blessing. Her pacifier seemingly moved in unison to his melodically soothing voice as he prayed over her and blessed her. While I savored every moment of the service, the highlight was watching my dad's now normally sullen face beam the entire time. We all assumed that this would be his last hurrah, and we were right. I'm thankful that I saw past the anxiety to gift him with the last best day of his life and provide the rest of the family with a beautiful memory.

A few weeks later, Morgan had a meltdown—better described as a shit fit—when my parents and in-laws came over to celebrate Rosh Hashanah. We'd just finished the blessing over the challah. As I sunk my teeth into a soft, fluffy slice, Morgan's juicy cheeks turned beet red. It was five o'clock on the dot, and she was revving up for her nightly freak out right on time. Ed and I sequestered ourselves in our bedroom to quietly rock Morgan while trying to calm her down. My mom came in offering, "Let me hold the baby, and you go eat." Then it was my mother-in-law Lenore's turn, "If you want, I'm happy to take Morgan overnight. Get some sleep and come pick her up tomorrow." My dad remained at the table while my father-in-law Morty kept him company. Stubbornness and first-time parent stupidity prevented me and Ed from accepting anyone's help. But if it was now, I'd answer, "Yes" to Lenore and add, "If you want, you can have her for the week." It felt like no other parents had a baby as difficult as ours. But when my friend described her son spraying the walls with projectile vomit, I thought, "Thank God I didn't have to deal with that."

A Desperation Called Motherhood

I would've given anything to quickly go back to work. But whenever I thought about it, I couldn't get past the guilt. What kind of mother returns to her job a few weeks after giving birth, especially when it's not for financial reasons? A bad mother, that's who. This no-win situation weighed heavily on my mind. As frustration grew, the rage I'd experienced from my mom took over. It stole my sanity and transformed me into a raging lunatic. I resented Ed for going to work every day while my life was dictated by a baby without a mute button. My saggy body disgusted me, I desperately craved a work routine, and I was miserable during what was supposed to be one of the happiest times in my life. Morgan's early evening fussy time was the most emotionally draining part of my day. I'd stressfully pick my finger until hearing the opening garage door announce Ed's arrival home from work. He often strolled in chirping, "Hello, my two girls. How was your day?" I'd throw Morgan in his arms the second he walked through the door and bitterly reply, "I know how your day was. You were with adults and not stuck in the goddam house." Ed noticed a drastic change in me from the moment that I became a mother. I'll never understand what stopped him from filing for divorce and demanding full custody.

A nearby support system would've made a huge difference. I wasn't asking much. Even crossing the street for a five-minute chat with a neighbor would've sufficed. But we lived in a predominantly Asian community where the neighbors didn't socialize with people outside their culture. There was no eye contact or neighborly wave hello during the few times that I caught a rare glimpse of someone. The one exception was our next-door neighbor. They were Italian, had children our age and seemed almost as delighted as our parents when Morgan made her grand debut. Having nowhere to go and no one to hang out with, Morgan and I often shared a good cry together. I can't count how many times I stared out the oversized front bay window and thought about how painfully lonely I was. Morgan didn't doze often—a half-hour nap was a hallelujah kind of day. So, I often walked around the block with her tucked into a snuggie to do what I called *airing out the baby*. A snuggie is a little carrier like a backpack, only you wear it in front to keep an eye on your little one. It's one of the best products that's ever hit the market. Getting out of the house felt like a reprieve from prison as I enjoyed the September balmy weather's calming effect. When I think back on that time in my life, the acute sense of hopelessness and loneliness that I experienced is eerily similar to how I felt before my suicide attempt.

When I'd finally reached my breaking point, I announced to Ed, "I can't stay home any longer." While he couldn't understand why I'd want to leave our beautiful baby when it wasn't necessary, he responded, "So, go back to work." I returned to work after three weeks—even though maternity leave covered six paid weeks. Coworkers looked at me oddly because no one expected me back so soon. When someone asked why I didn't stay home longer, I was embarrassed to say, "Work gave me the sanity and control I lost at home." I'd often say something evasive like, "It was easier this way." Receiving my first assignment symbolically handed me back my identity as a writer and a bit of much-needed control in my life. The professional part of Sharon never left, and not even a colicky baby or postpartum depression could break her spirit. But once again, guilt and self-loathing never failed to remind me that I didn't deserve to be a mother. On the other hand, it was healthy for Morgan to spend time during the week with our laid-back Jamaican nanny, Esmerelda. Going back to work also provided the space that I needed to appreciate family time on weekends. I've never had any regrets about returning to work so early because I did what was necessary, which was better for everyone.

Despite postpartum depression, I also experienced many wonderful times as a new mother. Since Morgan looked like a chunky buddha with the most pinchable cheeks, pretty much everything that she did was adorable. She let out a hearty laugh that came from the bottom of her soul, crawled on her butt like a crab and waved her arms up and down like a bird when she was excited. Ed and I referred to it as flapping. Even in my belly, Morgan kicked at the most inopportune times and often kept me up with hiccups that started the second I laid down. The last time that Ed placed his mouth on my swollen belly to sing a Grateful Dead song, she smacked him with a punch to the nose. She made her presence known even before she was born, and I had zero doubt that she'd be feisty like her mom.

Chapter 7

There's Nothing Good About a Final Goodbye

We took Morgan to my parent's house so that my dad could spend time with her while he was still alive. She'd lie in his arms while working out her chunky cheeks with her now mandatory pink and white pacifier. But she never closed her eyes. My dad was too busy staring at this little miracle and relishing every moment to fall asleep. I captured a picture of them lying in bed together, both content in a moment that's frozen in my mind for eternity.

My mom gave up a newly established real estate career to become my dad's caretaker. Many of their so-called friends stopped making plans because they couldn't deal with his mortality. Plus, having dinner at six o'clock instead of eight o'clock was an inconvenience they refused to accommodate. It was decades later when I recognized that most of my parent's friends abandoned them, which left my mom to deal with things alone. I didn't help matters. Since I wouldn't dare be mad at the person who was dying, I directed my anger toward my mom. In my mind, she could do no right, despite her saving my dad's life on more than one occasion. She understood where I was coming from and wisely walked away whenever I went on a rant. Toward the end of his illness, she stayed home to keep an eye on him while he pretty much slept 24/7. She told me, "I know your father is alive when I hear the toilet flush every morning." What an amusing yet sad observation. When my dad took over my bedroom, I was convinced that he did so because I was his favorite. But it probably didn't hurt that the room had its own private little bathroom.

Denial protected me from acknowledging my parent's sad existence. My mom was living a nightmare, and my dad didn't have the strength to leave the bedroom that he now referred to as his prison. On the other hand, my sister deserved a medal. She dealt amazingly well with the situation and probably visited my parents more than double the amount of times that I did. Whenever my mom desperately needed a break, my dad slept at Alyce's apartment. I was often overcome with guilt and jealousy because I couldn't find the strength that my sister had in spades. On top of that, she spent extra time with him while I protected myself by keeping my distance. During his last couple of years, my dad's liver was slowly shutting down. To this day, I can only envision him with bloodshot yellow eyes and the oddest army green colored skin. But what stands out most is his full head of black hair that won the battle against the gray to the very end.

A few months before my dad died, we attended a family bar mitzvah. He insisted on going even though he barely had the strength to put one foot in front of the other. It was obvious to everyone who saw him that he was close to dying. He was slowly staggering to his seat when he overheard an insensitive cousin loudly announce, "Murray looks horrible. I'm surprised he's still alive." This was the first time that I saw a resigned look in my dad's eyes. He was getting ready to face his death. My heart broke for him, but we chose not to confront the bigmouthed asshole and cause a scene. He eventually grew so weak that his energy was reserved for using the bathroom. When my dad no longer had the strength to even summon a hello during my visits, his half-closed adoring brown eyes always expressed how much he loved me. Visiting the house was now primarily for keeping my mom company or relieving her so that she could get out for a couple of hours.

My precious father lost his battle with myelofibrosis on March 9, 1995. A few days before his passing, my sister, Ed and Morgan ate breakfast with him at his favorite diner. As usual, I stayed home to catch an additional hour's sleep. But if I had even an inkling that he was going to refuse any more blood transfusions the following day, there's no way in hell that I would've slept in. Now that he required transfusions every other day, he said, "No more," which was code for, "I'm ready to die." Missing out on his last outing is one of my biggest regrets. On the other hand, I'm not sure if I could've kept my composure seeing him so close to death. As daddy's little girl, I'd been grieving his pending loss from the moment that I learned he was sick. Crying in front of him wouldn't exactly have given him a morale boost. I can imagine him sitting at the diner while quietly staring at Morgan and Alyce with his glassy yellow eyes—taking in the sight of his girls—minus me—for one last time. It's a haunting image that I wish I could erase from my mind. My dad didn't want to die with hospice in his so-called prison. So, once he refused any more transfusions, my mom admitted him to the hospital. When I visited him the day before he died, he was delirious from a lack of oxygen and determined to hop over the bed's metal railing. It took two badass security guards from Westchester County prison to hold him down. The last thing that I ever heard him say was, "Let me get up. I need to go to the fucking office." If you knew my dad, you'd understand why this was so appropriate and funny as hell. He'd have died sitting at his desk if my mom had been crazy enough to go along with his demented plan. Good or bad, I'm a lot like him, although I certainly wouldn't go so far as wanting to die at work.

 I'd already kissed him goodbye one hundred times and told him that I loved him a gazillion times more. So, when my mom called the next day urging, "Get to the hospital as soon as possible," I was tempted to sprint in the opposite direction. I wasn't emotionally ready to say goodbye to my favorite person in the entire world. As I headed from work toward a death I'd dreaded for years, I focused on the snow-covered homes and bare trees whizzing by the train's rain-stained window. As usual, I subconsciously picked my finger to alleviate the anxiety and adrenaline that was racing through my body. After jumping into my car at the train station and peeling out, I'm not sure if Mario Andretti could've kept up. It would've haunted me forever if I didn't get one last chance to say goodbye. As soon as I hurried through the hospital's entrance for about the fiftieth and last time, I headed straight for my dad's room. He couldn't communicate when I arrived, but he squeezed my hand to acknowledge my presence. Years later, a medium told me that he wanted so badly to say, "I love you." That one squeeze said it all and is as memorable as the first moment I laid eyes on my children.

My mom and Alyce headed to the hospital cafeteria to grab a bite to eat and give us some time alone. He was moaning and quickly rolling his head from side to side, which made it look like he was having a nightmare. But he'd squeezed my hand, so I knew that he heard me. While I tried reminiscing about happy and healthy times, I had to think really hard since he'd been sick for so long. I recalled, "Do you remember the time you fell and scraped your knee while teaching me how to ride a bike? You had to comfort your traumatized little five-year-old before tending to the blood dripping into your sneaker." I also nostalgically described us picking up our favorite "glazed, no jelly" donuts whenever I accompanied him to work. The man behind the counter knew to add two cups of tea with milk to the order, along with three sugar packets and plenty of napkins for me. It's amazing how simple, everyday routines can leave the most lasting impressions—and you don't even realize it until they're no longer a part of your life. Through flowing tears, I chuckled, "You know the wide rubber band where I wrote, 'I love you, fatso?' You showed it off to all your clients as if it was a rare coin worth a million bucks." Most parents show off pictures that their kids have drawn. But my dad was never typical—which is what I loved the most about him. Twenty minutes later, my mom and Alyce peaked inside the room with eyes asking for the latest update. He'd waited until their return so that he could die surrounded by his girls.

My sister and I held his left hand while mom sat on the right and soothed him, "It's okay to go, Murray. You put up one helluva fight."

This was the first time that I'd witnessed someone die, which made the experience even more surreal. The man dying in front of me was my father, my protector and my world. But I felt like a spectator who was watching a stranger take his last breath. I didn't purposely distance myself, but it helped me cope as I watched him slowly slip away. Alyce was crying hysterically and begging him not to leave while my mom unsuccessfully tried calming her down. At this point, his labored breaths had stopped synching with his barely moving chest. I selfishly wanted to speed up his death so that this nightmare would be over. Plus, I didn't want him to suffer any longer than he needed to. I'll never know if he was feeling pain, but there was no doubt that the three of us were in emotional agony.

My dad held on until I took a deep breath and whispered in his ear, "It's time to go, Daddy, we'll be okay. Go toward the light. I love you."

He adored both me and my sister, but I was the emotionally frail one all throughout his illness. For whatever reason, I knew that giving him *my* blessing would provide the strength he needed to leave. As my lips brushed against his prickly morning shadow, I gave him a little peck. A few minutes later, the moaning stopped right before we heard the death gurgle. My father had gone to a better place where illness, blood transfusions and pain ceased to exist. His jaundiced brown eyes remained wide open as he took his last breath. But when I tried closing them, they wouldn't budge. His shocked expression convinced me that he either saw the white light or encountered loved ones with outstretched arms welcoming him home.

My mom sprinted to the hall payphone to call the rabbi. She was working against the clock to arrange Dad's funeral before Shabbat, the next day before sundown. Otherwise, we'd have to wait until Sunday to bury him, prolonging the agony. Alyce and I offered to accompany her to the funeral home. But she told us to stay with my dad because she didn't want him feeling scared and alone. We followed his body all the way to the morgue, but before wheeling him in, the mortician said, "I'm sorry, but family isn't allowed to enter." It never seemed odd that we didn't want him to feel scared, even though I believe that his soul was no longer in his body.

After making funeral provisions, my mom rushed home to spread the news to family and friends. Since she always planned two steps ahead, this might've been the only time she was forced to make last-minute arrangements. She hired a shomer, which derives from an old Jewish tradition where someone stays with the body to protect it from evil spirits and ensure that it's treated with dignity and respect. The shomer also cleansed and prepared my dad's body for burial before praying over him throughout the night. While I don't necessarily believe in God, I think Jewish traditions are beautiful and often incorporate them into my life.

The next day, about twenty-five people showed up to help us wish my dad goodbye. We expected it to be an intimate gathering, especially since it was taking place on such short notice. Everyone commented on his dry sense of humor, and my friends rehashed memories of his generosity. Buying hard-to-get *The Who* concert tickets and taking us to his favorite restaurant in Chinatown beforehand was just one of the infinite examples. I didn't realize at the time how precious that dinner was to him, but as a parent, I certainly do now.

Right before the service, I needed one last kiss. Jews don't normally open the casket, but in the back room, I poked my head deep inside and whispered two inches away from his now clean-shaven face. As I told him, "I love you so much, I already miss you," the tears that were blurring my eyes poured down my cheeks and landed on his cool stiff cheek. Burying him with my intimate tears was an accidental, yet beautiful, way to eternally say, "I love you." This was the first time that I'd visited my parent's pre-purchased burial site. As I looked around, I loved how the tall bushy trees framed the perimeter of the entire cemetery. While the rabbi prayed at the short burial service, I didn't want to believe that the man whom I adored was in that plain wooden coffin, never to be seen or hugged again. At the end of the service, it's a Jewish tradition for each immediate family member to shovel dirt on top of the coffin. Then other loved ones and friends do the same before the funeral home's ground crew completes the task. I can't remember if I put a handful of dirt on the coffin, but I definitely didn't use a shovel. Since that day, the sound of dirt raining down on other people's coffins always takes me back to my dad—and the vision that I created of his bones lying in the ground. I have no idea who gave the eulogy—for all I know, it could've been me. Many experiences during his dying days are still very clear, yet a large part of his funeral is a complete blur.

Toward the end of his life, my dad insisted, "I don't want you visiting my dead bones." I took those words to heart and have only visited the cemetery around five times in twenty-two years. During one of those visits, I brought my children to share stories of their Poppy while showing them his tall black tombstone. They ran around the cemetery, politely greeting my dad's fellow graveyard mates. If he saw us from heaven, I can imagine him bragging to his fellow spirits, "That's my daughter and grandchildren, aren't they beautiful?" On his tombstone is etched, "Life isn't forever, love is." I cherish those words and use them to comfort others during their time of grief because nothing truer has ever been said. If he was alive during my worst depression, even my dad couldn't have saved me from the last ten years until I was ready to save myself. But I do believe that the only reason I survived was because he refused to let me die. In retrospect, perhaps he did save me after all. As a medium once told me, "Your dad says that it wasn't your time."

In the Jewish religion, the immediate family is expected to sit Shiva for seven days, beginning right after the funeral. During this time, the immediate family remains at home and sits on low boxes or stools to reinforce their inner emotions of "feeling low." Upon returning home from the cemetery, a pitcher of water is placed outside the house so that visitors can show respect and honor for the dead by washing their hands before entering. All the mirrors in the house are covered because this is supposed to be a time of self-reflection when mourners aren't expected to worry or care about their appearance.

That afternoon, friends and family heaped the dining room table with arms full of typical kosher deli meats, kugel, brisket and sweets. After unloading their goodies, they would predictably head toward the three of us and say, "I'm so sorry for your loss. He's in a better place." I wanted to throw a tantrum and scream, "Being dead wasn't a better place than being here with his family. He never should've been terminally ill at such a young age and unable to see his grandchildren grow up." Instead, I used Morgan as an excuse to sometimes hide in my room. Seeing everyone gather around my mom made me cringe because her emotional pain and vulnerability were more than I could handle.

On the second day of Shiva, I woke up with a bad case of bronchitis. My body was as stressed as my mind, and it inevitably had a meltdown. I left Morgan sitting in the hallway of my mom's home to entertain visitors with her flapping and screeching while I rushed to the emergency clinic. Given how sick I was, it was going to become a true emergency if I didn't begin taking antibiotics. As I sat in the waiting room, an older gentleman lost his footing as he bent over to take a sip from the water fountain. People began staring at me when, seemingly out of nowhere, I began bawling like a baby. The man's weakness reminded me of my dad.

Ed was knee-deep in a high-profile project at work and would've got stuck pulling all-nighters if he spent the day sitting Shiva. Feeling guilty and not wanting to be an inconvenience, I said, "Go to the office, I'm fine." And I meant it. But trying to avoid being an inconvenience, no matter how negatively it affected me, extended to my loved ones. People had better things to do, so I never asked for help unless I had no choice. I'm pretty sure that I inherited my not wanting to burden anyone from my mother. But it becomes exhausting when you're forced to do everything on your own. I thought I'd handled my dad's death well until years later when I realized that I'd dealt with it by not dealing with it. The best way to describe it is putting my sadness in an imaginary box, locking it up tight and wrapping it ten times over with heavy metal chains. By the time I attempted suicide, my demons had somehow ripped opened the box and convinced me that I didn't deserve to live. When I began believing them, evil had won.

Being alone for the first time in her life, my mom asked if she could arrange a weekly visit with Morgan. But my repressed sadness clouded my empathy, and my anger made me say no. I should've seen how difficult it must've been for her to be married at eighteen and widowed at fifty-seven. This goes to the very top of my list of shitty things that I wish I could take back. It's amazing how many sad things I forbade my brain from processing. I once blamed it on selfishness, but I now understand that deep empathy often makes me too vulnerable to cope. To avoid feeling other people's sorrow, and my own, I'd either shut down with depression or become a raging lunatic. Undoubtedly, I preferred depressed Sharon to the irrational, shrieking one.

Chapter 8

Growing Pains and Gains

When you already know what to expect, the second time around seems so much easier. I've heard it's that way with marriage too.

Ed and I planned on having two children. But now that every little thing set me off, I wasn't sure if I could handle a second baby. I also feared a repeat of nausea, a split pelvis, trouble breathing and postpartum depression. Staring at me with puppy dog eyes, Ed proclaimed, "But you promised." Unable to refuse, I suffered for another nine long months and added dizzy spells and fainting fits to my list of ailments. But despite all my aches and pains, my second pregnancy wasn't as tough as the first. Myles Alexander Greenwald was born on October 21, 1996. It was and always will be the only time that I've experienced love at first sight. My funny-looking baby was white as a ghost with meconium on his face, big ears like Dumbo and a comical red birthmark under his big nose that resembled Hitler's mustache. Having my tubes tied two hours after giving birth meant that the hospital kept us admitted for an additional three days of peace and quiet. Postpartum depression eluded me this time around, and Myles was the happiest, most easy-going little guy.

But the honeymoon was over after bringing him home because Morgan didn't appreciate sharing us with her funny-looking baby brother. After introducing her to Myles, she curiously tilted her face, touched his fuzzy bald head and tottered away. When the family arrived to visit the following day, they ignored Myles to dote on Morgan. We wanted her to feel like the most important person in the world. Despite the attention everyone showered on her, Morgan quickly began acting out. It didn't help matters when Ed decided that it was somehow a good idea to put her in a big girl bed while she was still adjusting to our new addition to the family. He made the situation even worse by telling her that the crib was now for Myles. I completely disagreed with the lousy timing, but when Ed made up his mind about something, he wouldn't budge. We didn't sleep for the following two nights, thanks to his asinine timing. Many of our fights were centered around our two different parenting styles and continued even after the divorce.

Myles now occupied the last free room in our cramped twelve hundred square foot home. Before his birth, I was using the room to speed walk on my treadmill. Initially, the compromise was for me to exercise in the wee hours of the morning while Myles slept in his crib. On those days when I unintentionally woke him up, I laid him in Ed's arms for what became father/son bonding time. Since working out grounded me on a daily basis and I couldn't take over Myles' bedroom forever, Ed knew that it was time to upgrade to a larger house. When we mentioned moving while visiting close friends in Briarcliff Manor, they gave us a tour of their quaint town. Ed and I loved the rustic winding roads, majestic one-hundred-year-old oak trees, and eclectic mixture of cottages and mansions. Our decision to set down roots there was sealed upon hearing about the award-winning school system. While the real estate agent schlepped us around to at least ten houses, Ed couldn't find a chef's kitchen with the top-notch stainless-steel appliances that he coveted. I wasn't willing to sacrifice walk-in closets that could accommodate the wardrobe of someone who didn't wear the same outfit twice. That's when we decided to build a home that included all the amenities we wanted. In March 1997, we settled into our forty-five hundred square foot Asian-styled home that sat on an acre of lush green land. It could've been featured in House Beautiful with its pagoda facade, tremendously high ceilings, wall-to-wall windows, chef's kitchen and closets the size of a Manhattan studio. It was a great decision because we loved the house, the town and the lifelong friends we'd make along the way.

Our nanny didn't want to commute to the burbs; it was too far from her apartment in Queens. So, we hired a new caregiver named Liz. Perhaps my brain and vibe meter were stuck in baby hormone fog because she turned out to be a doozy of a mistake. Liz adored Myles, but what I didn't discover until later is that she essentially ignored Morgan. One day when I was home to pick up Morgan from her Montessori preschool, the teacher called me over. She suspected that Liz wasn't treating Morgan well because "Your nanny isn't warm to Morgan and she walks so fast to the car that Morgan has to run to keep up." Upon receiving this piece of news, we immediately threw Liz out of the house. I warned Sarah and Slim, a couple we'd hired to design and plant our backyard garden, "Don't be alarmed if you see a new person. We were told yesterday that Liz wasn't treating Morgan well, so we kicked her out." That's when they confessed, "I'm glad. We've seen Liz do mean things to Morgan." When I asked for an example, Sarah commented, "Liz went into the house with Myles and let the door slam in Morgan's face." I responded in disbelief, "Why didn't you tell me sooner? I would've believed you and never held it against you." They were afraid of getting involved, as Sarah explained, "We didn't want to say anything because we didn't know how you'd react or if you'd get mad at us." But I'm not one of those parents who conveniently denies the truth if it means disrupting my life. If I had to stay home for a week or two until we found a new nanny, I would've gladly done it for the sake of my little girl. I've never forgiven myself for not sensing that Morgan was being mistreated. If I didn't work, this never would've happened. Of course, I added this experience to my growing list of mistakes that I'd made as a shitty mother.

No matter where I went, my issues stuck with me like my shadow. But a fortuitous reprieve provided years of happiness, despite my looming demons. This was probably the best time in my life, and I never realized it until now. Our new nanny, Jemma, was referred to us by her friend Brenda who worked down the street. Brenda quickly introduced her to a circle of nannies who all hung out together while on playdates with the kids. I became fast friends with one of the kid's moms when a one-minute question turned into an hour phone conversation that ended with, "It was great talking to you. Let's make plans with the kids for next weekend." During my first get-together with a few moms from the group, each woman was nicer than the last. I relished the times that we spent with and without the kids. Postpartum depression might not have kicked my ass if I'd lived here when Morgan was born. Our group consisted of six couples, with friends of friends joining us at any given time. At the town pool, I was always prepared to welcome a newcomer with, "Here, let me make some room for you and the kids." The adults looked forward to hanging out at the pool as much as the kids did.

Around the same time, I ran into my next-door neighbor while hiking up my long driveway to get the mail. Unlike our first house, I hoped against hope that I'd form deep connections with people in the neighborhood. It was obvious by her standoffish vibe that Lisa was selective with whom she let into her life. But I was determined to win over this attractive blond with the mischievous smile. We were caught up in a conversation when Ed put Myles on the roof of my parked car and walked away. Of course, he was safely strapped in his baby carrier, but it still wasn't the ideal place to leave an infant. That was Ed's way of saying, "Here, you take care of the baby for a while." After a few minutes, Lisa asked, "Uh, do you know your son is on top of the car?" I'd caught sight of the carrier from the corner of my eye. But we had a good laugh when Lisa commented, "Oh my God, my husband Robert would've done the same thing. They're two peas in a pod." Right then, I knew that I'd won her over. We continued our long chitchat at dinner with our husbands the following evening. Our friendship quickly blossomed into best friends. She became my confidante and cheerleader, the neighbor I hung out with during snowstorms and Halloween and my crisis counselor. I easily formed relationships with many other people in our predominantly young parent, upscale town. Nancy and I were becoming acquainted during the commute to work, while her daughter Jessica and Morgan were simultaneously becoming besties at elementary school. When Morgan mentioned Nancy's last name, I said, "That's so funny, I already know her. Let's make plans." The four of us enjoyed many mommy-daughter dinners and once traveled upstate together for a long weekend.

Four years after moving to Briarcliff Manor, I was introduced to Sharon, another one of Morgan's friend's mom. Sharon and I instantly bonded and always referred to ourselves as female soulmates—I sincerely believe that we knew each other in a past life. At the time, I didn't have a clue that our special friendship would eventually break my heart. Around town, my friend Sharon was known as Sharon One, and I was anointed Sharon Two. I loved sharing my name with my best friend, which solidified the belief that we were meant to be in each other's lives. Morgan became best friends with Sharon's daughter Samantha and referred to Sharon as her second mother. Going out with a friend to dinner or a movie is a nice part of any relationship. But Sharon and I sincerely loved each other and shared a much deeper connection. Our friendship was based on calling each other twice a day and my keeping her company while she drove her autistic twins to school. When depression took the life out of me, Sharon was the only one who could get me out of the house and convince me to eat. We were friends to the core and often laughed so hard in the car that Sharon couldn't catch her breath. Whenever I had to grab her asthma inhaler out of her bag, we laughed even harder. By having an amazing group of friends, I never felt alone. While the anger always festered just below the surface, contentment successfully battled my demons on most days—allowing me to enjoy the best phase of my married life.

Every Saturday morning, Ed took the kids out for breakfast while I slept in. There aren't many men who'd even consider taking a newborn and a two-year-old to a restaurant alone. Especially when the two-year-old could scream louder than the top ten heavy metal singers. Many friends were jealous because their husbands never did half of the things that Ed did as a hands-on dad. I'd usually wake up before they returned home and use the opportunity to clean up the house. Given my obsession with control, it wasn't always easy having a house that wasn't in perfect order. I often stepped on GI Joe's face in the shower and, more than once, found open magic markers stuffed between the couch pillows in the den. With two youngsters, my home wasn't going to be immaculate, and the only option was making peace with my neurosis. Most of the time I could deal with the clutter, and many people wouldn't have considered the house messy. But since having my colicky Morgan, losing control became a trigger.

After my dad died, I continually locked my uncomfortable feelings in my safe box. But like a dam that's about to burst, the overflowing water had to spill somewhere. Instead of processing things properly, my tension was released in the form of rage and picking my finger. Whenever something set me off, it felt like a faceless fiend was taking over my mind and body. The anger started at my toes and rapidly worked its way up until my head felt like a raw egg that was about to explode in someone's tight fist. Its fury scared the hell out of me, but there was no controlling it. If you asked Ed, I'm pretty sure he'd say that this was what he loathed most about me.

One of my more noteworthy breakdowns occurred after taking an hour's drive to see friends on Long Island. We couldn't find the house because I'd forgotten to take their address and phone number. Before cell phones had Internet, there was no way of looking up the information unless we somehow found a printed phonebook. Ed drove around in circles for fifteen minutes while ignoring my pleas to get back on the highway and go home. I tried grabbing the wheel a couple of times, but Ed shoved my arm away with such force that he gave me a bruise. This pissed me off even more, especially since I now had zero control over the situation. When he began slowing down for a stop sign, I threw the gear into park and killed the transmission on my brand-new Infiniti. When we weren't fighting over our two very different parenting styles, Ed and I predominantly clashed about my anger. I was petrified seeking help because if therapy didn't work, I'd have nowhere else to turn. Instead, I apologized every time I lost my shit, which, after a while, became way too often. Not seeking help for fear of failure is common for people who suffer from depression. It's amazing how depressed people share identical thoughts and actions, regardless of what precipitates the sadness.

The kids often got involved in our fights, which triggered my rage even more. Ed wouldn't back me up when I pointed out that they were overstepping boundaries, and I found his laissez-faire attitude disrespectful. This was a touchy subject, and it was a big reason why I often felt like a second-class citizen in my own home. Not being on the same page with our parenting styles played one of the biggest roles in tearing us apart.

If I knew then what I know now, I would've sought help sooner. My family deserved better—and I did too. Instead, the kids lived on pins and needles during their early years with the same tension that I endured with my mom.

Sick and Sicker

Sinus infections, which became as predictable as the kids storming into our room every weekend at the break of dawn, added to my emotional woes.

Myles was born with asthma, which made him prone to sinus infections. They supposedly aren't contagious, but he and I constantly came down with them, so take what you will from that. When my infection became resistant to regular antibiotics, I was prescribed Trovan. At the time, it was one of the most potent antibiotics on the market. Seemingly out of nowhere, I couldn't move my left shoulder and needed two cortisone shots for what the doctor diagnosed as bursitis. I didn't give it a second thought until years later when I found myself once again scrunching up my face in agony every time I put on a shirt. Trovan was taken off the market after people began dying from liver failure. It was replaced with Levaquin, another now-controversial antibiotic from the fluoroquinolone group of drugs. Levaquin was relatively new, and little did I know that each pill was tearing my body—and my sanity—apart. After a year of popping pills for a sinus infection that wouldn't quit, my ENT scanned my three-inch chart and proclaimed, "We can't put surgery off any longer, you're very sick." I wish he'd come to that conclusion sooner because the drugs had already turned my tendons to mush. The operation successfully opened my nasal passageway and eliminated the infection. After a year of physical hell, I erroneously thought that I could finally put the suffering behind me. But I couldn't have been more wrong.

Adding Injury to Insult

When an achy ankle sent me to the surgeon, I was expecting him to give me the all-clear while possibly advising, "Give the treadmill a rest for a week or two, and see if your ankle feels better."

The pain was tolerable, and I'd only made an appointment because it was throbbing right above a scar where the doctor had removed a floating bone years earlier. Upon returning a week later for the MRI results, I couldn't stop picking my finger when the doctor summoned me over to look at the scans. I said, "No, I'm not looking, that means it's bad news." Nodding with a surprised expression, he replied, "It is, your Achilles tendon is completely torn from top to bottom." Since I'm as athletic as an eighty-year-old with fasciitis, I questioned in shock, "How could this happen? I didn't injure myself." The doctor simply shrugged his shoulders and sent me out front to schedule an appointment for surgery. This was a turning point when damage from the strong antibiotics I'd repeatedly taken for sinus infections began punishing me with yearly tendon surgery. I was already emotionally drained, and the addition of physical trauma was enough to send me from merely existing to fighting to survive the ocean's unrelenting undertow.

Two weeks post-diagnosis, I found myself sitting alone in the hospital bay, waiting for a nurse to escort me to the operating room.

Sixty-ninth Street Suicide

My eyes roamed from curtain to curtain as I counted how many other pre-op patients were by themselves. The tears came fast and steady upon realizing that I was the only one without a support person. Luckily, I was able to avoid asking someone to go out of their way and pick me up in the city. Going in, I hopped on the first Metro North train at 5 a.m. Our au pair, who I had no problem asking for help, drove me home. She dropped me off by the stone path that started about fifty feet from my front door. Then she drove back to Ed's house to wait for the kids to return from school. Being on my own within six hours of surgery, I fell *up* the stairs and onto my big left toe that was poking out of my knee-high cast. Since a pain-reducing drug called Marcaine was injected to numb my ankle for about twenty-four hours, I couldn't immediately determine if I'd caused any damage. But the next day, I was tempted to smash the hard white cast against a rock when my swollen foot and ankle rubbed against the stiff, unforgiving plaster. Since I didn't want to inconvenience the doctor over the weekend, I waited four excruciating days to schedule an emergency appointment. Every intolerable second felt like someone was rubbing sandpaper on an open wound.

If I was going to have any chance of sleeping through the pain, popping an Ambien was the only solution. But a year earlier, I'd blacked out on one Ambien pill and scared the hell out of Myles by screaming in his face, "I'm high, I'm high." I considered it my way of scaring him straight, which I'd later discover wasn't particularly effective. Mixing Ambien with my daily meds didn't sit well with my fear of going crazy or becoming violently ill while I was immobile. When the need for sleep won out, I tossed my medication for depression to the side. Since I didn't consciously feel any different the next day without it, I presumed that my depression had been cured. Boy, was I wrong and naive! Struggling alone in Sharon's world, I thought that I could handle everything on my own. Looking back from a healthier perspective, it was like throwing the oars out of a boat and kidding myself that it would be equally effective if I used my arms to paddle.

When Ed picked up the kids to ring in 2007, he stuck his head in my room to see how I was feeling. He found me thrashing from side to side in pain and offered, "Do you want me to stay with you?" Saying yes wasn't fair, so I took an Ambien and slept through midnight. When the doctor sawed off the cast during my emergency appointment a couple of days later, the bottom of my foot was black. It reminded me of what dying flesh from frostbite looks like, which I'd seen on my favorite medical shows. He commented while shaking his head, "This isn't good, what did you do?" I'd been bleeding internally for four days, which led to my ankle swelling in the cast and magnifying the pain tenfold.

As if this experience wasn't bad enough, I would require future surgeries—including the ankle that was previously operated on. Needing eight surgeries in twelve years took a heavy toll. It didn't help matters that the timing synched with my separation. When I think back on my ten-year depression, suffering alone from surgery after surgery is one of the first horrors that comes to mind.

Chapter 9

Making Work, Work

When I met Ed at the age of twenty-eight, I was like Peggy Olson from the *Mad Men* series. Peggy Olson—a female copywriter clawing her way to the top in the Big Apple. Leaving my career to become a stay-at-home mom never once crossed my mind.

Ed preferred that I stop working to raise the kids, which his successful banking career readily accommodated. When I announced, "There's no way I'm not going back to work, I love writing," he acquiesced, saying, "Fine. But you're in charge of the kids during the week. I can't take time off so that you can go to work." Since copywriting wasn't nearly as demanding as Ed's career, I easily balanced work with family life for seven years. Our dependable live-in nanny Dorestine took good care of the kids and made it possible for me to continue working. I was always on call if one of them became sick or got hurt, and I took time off for special events. When the kids brought home a note from school requesting trip chaperones, I reminded them at least three times the following morning to hand in the signed form. But without missing a beat, they would whine, "I don't want you going on the school trip. You're not fun." This always made me feel like shit. I wasn't a strict parent, and I loved doing fun things out of the ordinary with them, like having dessert at Carvel before dinner. While growing up, I was lucky if I got Carvel *after* dinner.

But in Ed's and the kid's eyes, I could do no right. Even when I did something special, it seemed to go unnoticed. When I set up a last-minute driving lesson on Morgan's sweet sixteen, after her paternal grandfather unexpectedly died four days earlier, no one acknowledged what a thoughtful gesture it was. I never scored bonus points for all the positive things that I did because all anyone could focus on was my rage. This continued for years, even after I got my anger under control—it was like being unable to shake a stereotype. On the other hand, the kids knew that they could always count on me for support. I loved my mommy bear role, which came in handy since Ed did everything possible to avoid confrontation. If anyone tried messing with my kids, they had me to deal with. My support seemed to give Morgan and Myles the confidence that they needed to stand up for themselves.

My writing career fulfilled a part of me that nothing else could. Never did I think that anything could make me leave advertising until one day when the world changed…

September 11, 2001

It was a beautiful crisp Tuesday morning with the sky as clear and crystal blue as the Caribbean Sea. I hopped off the packed train at Grand Central and impatiently waited in the predictably long line for my morning chocolate chip muffin. Afterward, I headed to work right across the street on Forty-Second Street and Lexington Avenue.

People were hustling and bustling and pushing each other like any other typical morning in New York City—especially when the white blinking light indicated that it was safe to cross the street. But after stepping off the elevator at work, it transformed into the worst day in American history. At 8:46 on the morning of September 11, 2001, the first plane hit the World Trade Center's north tower. Upon strolling into the office about ten minutes later, I learned what had happened. Like everyone else, I dismissed it as an accident. But when a second plane smashed into the south tower at 9:03 a.m., we stopped misconstruing the first crash as a random event. The United States was under attack, and my beloved city was the main target. Fifteen coworkers joined me in the only conference room with a TV to watch the drama unfold. Despite my office being located fifty blocks away from the towers, the large south-facing conference room window provided a front-row view of death, destruction and hate. The horror and terror of watching an attack in New York City felt like a scene out of *Homeland*. After the first tower went crashing down, everyone in the room remained staring at the TV screen as if in a trance. Their faces were stoic, and they seemed curiously calm. For me, it was incredibly real witnessing one of New York's most iconic landmarks burst into flames, rain 107 stories of debris around downtown Manhattan and instantly turn the World Trade Center into a graveyard.

My reaction was to scream, "Oh my God, all those people just died." Everyone's expression now transformed into shock and panic. This wasn't a movie they were watching, and those people still trapped in the second tower were probably doomed to a similar fate. Even worse, there was not a damn thing that anyone could do to save them. Before the first tower collapsed, I was convinced that helicopters would land on the roof to rescue those who were trapped above the fire. But now I held my breath as I anticipated a repeat of one of the most God-awful images I'd ever witness. Sure enough, we watched the second tower crumble soon afterward and take an important piece of New York City with it. Convinced that the terrorists had additional plans for us that day, everyone scrambled to call loved ones and figure out the next steps. We were panicking and aimlessly running around each other in circles. Exclamations like "The phone lines are jammed" or "My friend works in that building" could be heard up and down the long narrow hall. In addition, "Oh my God, oh my God," was repeated over and over like a mantra.

Ed was working at the Traveler's building, which was three blocks north of the towers. At the time, I wasn't sure how close he was to the mayhem. If I'd known, I probably would've had what my therapist calls catastrophic thoughts—which means focusing on the worst-case scenario. In this instance, I might've imagined Ed bleeding to death after being smacked in the head by flying debris. After the first tower fell, I tried calling him to see what we should do. But I couldn't get through because all the phone lines in New York—and the entire country—were jammed. I then tried emailing him on his Blackberry, which was never far from his thumbs. No surprise, he immediately replied. We agreed that I would walk crosstown, where Ed would pick me up in his car and look for any way possible to get the hell out of NYC. There wasn't a vehicle on the road, and only one or two people were within sight. So, I quickly strode down the double middle yellow line on Forty-Second Street. The silence on the empty streets was spooky. Our conversation in the car was manic as Ed plotted how to get us far away from the insanity. We both held our breath while racing to the 125th Street bridge, which Ed determined was our best chance. Despite the media saying that NYC was on lockdown, the bridge became our savior. With a huge sigh of relief, we hightailed it back to Westchester.

Ed worked from home the next few days while his debris-filled building was closed. Out of sheer terror, I hid within the confines of my home's four walls. I spent practically every minute watching the towers fall again and again on TV. It felt like I was waiting for a different, happier ending that would never come. At some point, Ed commented, "Stop watching that. I don't want the kids to keep seeing it." As an intensely empathetic person, 9/11 brought up many conflicting emotions for me as unimaginable pain overtook the nation. They aren't just words when I tell the kids, "I wish I could take away your pain and give it to me." I'd rather be the one suffering than watch someone else in misery while I'm powerless to help. Reacting this way about loved ones and strangers alike has caused me a great deal of angst all throughout my life.

I must've watched the same video of people jumping at least one hundred times and cringed when imagining what they must've been thinking and feeling. I'm terrified of heights. So, I decided that if it were me, I would've slit my wrists to die quicker and avoid any more pain from the smoke and heat. If Ed was killed, I envisioned holding up his photo and marching alongside everyone else who'd lost a loved one. 9/11 also presented an opportune time to kill myself. Since I didn't work near the towers, I created a scenario of walking downtown and inserting myself where I had a good chance of being killed. That way, I could die without anyone knowing that it was intentional. I feel horribly guilty sharing these thoughts when nearly three thousand innocent victims would've done anything to survive.

After a long, solemn week, I gathered up the nerve to resume my work routine. As soon as the airports reopened, a few of us traveled to Washington, DC, for a meeting with our clients from the post office. On the way there, I witnessed the damage firsthand while flying directly over the Pentagon. Returning home, the flight took us over the still smoldering remains of what was once the World Trade Center. In an odd way, viewing the sites firsthand helped a part of me stop obsessing about what had happened.

I was also confronted with the reality of 9/11 every night when I caught my usual 5:29 Harlem train home to the security of the suburbs. I'd begun allotting extra time because I knew that I had to make a pit stop before dashing for the train on platform twenty-six on the upper level. A special whiteboard was set up in Grand Central for people to post pictures of lost loved ones. Every smiling face of mothers, fathers, siblings, friends and spouses shared the same tragic header: "Have you seen him/her?" We all knew the answer, but no one dared to break the chain of hope by responding with the unthinkable truth. I was drawn in every time I walked past the board. Once again, death and suffering sent me to a place where most people seldom ventured.

The people staring back at me were strangers until the day I glimpsed a familiar face. I couldn't immediately place the dark man with the distinctive thick eyebrows until I shockingly realized he was my train guy—an Indian gentleman who always sat two seats in front of me on the way home. In that instant, my top priority became being home with the kids. I loved working, but I loved my family a whole lot more, and the man on the train reminded me of where my priorities lay. There was also a concrete reason why sticking close to home was so important. I was convinced that the terrorists weren't done with us yet, and I didn't want the kids to become orphaned if Ed and I were both victims of a second attack. Plus, working in a corner office that faced Grand Central Station had become an issue. Every time I caught a looming shadow from my large office window of a military plane scouring the area, I darted into the hall. The day that I slammed into my boss and nearly knocked him over, he suggested that I take a break. Even better, I decided to take a hiatus from advertising altogether and focus on being a mom. One of the best decisions that I've ever made was leaving a fulfilling, high-paying job to watch over my then five- and seven-year-olds.

Choosing to stay home meant that our beloved nanny Dorestine was no longer needed to watch the kids. She was a kind, godly person who treated Morgan and Myles as if they were her own. Ed was very matter-of-fact about the situation and tried reassuring me, "Why are you so upset, she'll be fine. We gave her a plane ticket to visit her family in London and she'll find another job when she gets back. If she needs a recommendation, we'll give her a great one." But I was more upset than the kids because I've always found saying goodbye agonizingly difficult. I was sad to see Dorestine go, and I felt guilty that it was my fault she no longer had a job. My tremendous sensitivity is one of the reasons why I'd make a dreadful boss.

I was warned that transitioning from the working world to being a stay-at-home mom is one of life's most stressful challenges. But thanks to my lucrative hobby, everything went smoothly. When I made the decision to stop working, I was already selling the kid's old wardrobes on eBay. I also sold clothing and collectibles for friends and envisioned turning my eBay store into a small consignment shop. By filling up my time selling wares online, I ensured that staying home with the kids would remain an emotionally healthy decision.

As a copywriter, it was a cinch creating a simple marketing plan to advertise my services. The first step was identifying the most popular high-end magazine in my area. *Westchester Magazine* targeted upscale readers primarily earning $100,000 and up. Within a week of advertising, people began responding to my modest 3 x 5, upper right-hand corner ad. Building a small business was a gratifying endeavor. Plus, there was no way I'd ever be okay sitting at home eating bonbons all day while Ed worked his butt off. According to eBay, I've successfully grossed about seven hundred and fifty thousand dollars since 1999. But the best part was that it occupied my time while the kids were at school.

A Beautiful Memory

A week after 9/11, I was on crutches after having surgery to remove a floating bone in my ankle. Given my lack of balance, remaining vertical was both a challenge and a miracle.

While I was on my way to the surgeon for a follow-up appointment a couple of weeks later, my shoelace had come undone. Bending down to retie it would've meant endangering my face, so I figured that I'd get to it when I had a chance to sit down. But as I approached the hospital, a woman noticed my long laces and, without saying a word, bent down to tie them. It was one of the most beautiful moments in my life and a memorable display of kindness at its best.

Trixie

Whenever I spot a dog, my impulse is to drop everything and run over to squish their furry beards. If the owner gives me permission to pet said dog, I get on all fours and speak to them in my baby voice. I can relate when someone says that they love dogs more than people because I do, too.

I'd always dreamt of adding a dog to the family but working full-time meant that I'd have to pass on the responsibility to our nanny. Dorestine didn't even believe in letting a dog stay in the house, so that idea was quashed. Leaving my job freed up the time needed for me to properly train a puppy. While traveling to the tip of Long Island to meet our Wheaton Terrier, the kids excitedly anticipated who she'd like more and who she'd sleep with. In the end, the answer to both questions was me. Despite the breeder's website stressing a two-year waiting list, my inspirational email convinced her that our wait was over before it even began. All I needed to do was speak from the heart about how I'd always wanted a Wheaton Terrier and what kind of loving home we'd give her. Ed often seemed embarrassed that I wore my heart on my sleeve, but he knew what he was getting into pretty much from our first date. As we headed toward the breeder's modest one-level home, the crunching of dead leaves underneath our feet announced our arrival. The house was set far back in the woods of Montauk, surrounded by bare trees that had shed their greenery a month earlier. When I rang the doorbell, the feeling of serenity was broken with the sound of dogs barking in unison. After introducing ourselves and speaking with the breeder for a few minutes, she told us to get ready to meet two female pups. We were gathered in a circle on the floor when two tiny adorable soft-coated fur balls with black faces and stubby tails came barreling over to us. As we oohed and aahed, one puppy went straight to me, flicked her little tongue on my hand and made her way around the room. The other one ran around in circles like a maniac. At that moment, we welcomed our calm little Trixie to the family. Little did I know that years later, she'd help me stay alive before breaking my heart. Whenever I listed items on eBay, Trixie made herself comfortable by stretching out on the pile of clothing that was always next to my feet. I relished how she often stared at me with her adoring brown puppy dog eyes. Having someone to keep me company—even if it was a dog who couldn't respond to our one-sided conversations—helped to prevent me from becoming lonely.

    Staying home without a formal routine was both a nightmare and a blessing when my depression hit in the summer of 2005. I'd sit at my work desk, frozen in place for hours, while staring at the ceiling. Holding down a regular job would've been essentially impossible. But as a creature of habit, a routine might've forced me out of the house and helped me to function. I had twenty-four hours a day to be depressed and took advantage of every suffocating minute.

Chapter 10

The Beginning of the End

In 2005, Morgan and Myles were eight and ten, respectively, when they went to sleepaway camp. Being alone with Ed again for the first time in almost a decade, I assumed that we'd enjoy a second mini honeymoon and strengthen our relationship.

Instead, we lived parallel lives with Ed playing golf while I hung out with friends at our country club's pool. I'd already distanced myself emotionally with anger and sadness, and now I was physically pushing him away. My brain had no idea what was going on, but when my body shut down and began dropping weight, I knew something was terribly wrong.

My journey began when a hot twenty-something man, who looked like a younger version of Harry Connick Jr., hit on me. Nothing happened, but his attention stirred up complex emotions, and anxiety stole my appetite. Even though my shocking weight loss was a cause for concern, I still didn't realize that depression was triggering what I'd self-diagnosed as a nervous breakdown. Instead, I concluded that my drastic physical transformation was the result of a midlife crisis—specifically, the need to be with another man. I'd never disrespect Ed by cheating, so in October, I asked him for permission to have a fling. He shrugged his shoulders and muttered, "Do what you need to do." His response simultaneously caused a feeling of relief and rejection. If a man truly loves his wife, he doesn't send her off to be intimate with another man. But then, I always questioned how deeply Ed truly loved me. I'm not sure if it was paranoia, if he wasn't an expressive or affectionate man or if he liked me more than he loved me. On the other hand, if Ed had said no, I'm not sure how I would've handled my breakdown. My conflicted feelings never made sense to anyone but me, and my question undoubtedly caught Ed off guard. But he'd been watching me wither away for months, and he would've done anything to get back the angry, but functioning, mother of his children.

Having been out of the singles scene for fourteen years, I was both psyched and shocked upon discovering a dating website that catered specifically to married people. Ashley Madison was the go-to place for people who wanted to discretely arrange an affair. For me, having a fling with a married man was safer—especially since I never thought that my midlife crisis would result in divorce. Pete was the first man with whom I corresponded. Since he lived three thousand miles away in Los Angeles, I figured that there was a minuscule chance we'd ever meet. But I quickly began relying on this stranger for validation. Pete texted me every day at exactly three o'clock NY time, with the first message alert making my heart jump with excitement. I'd quickly respond before staring at the screen, waiting for the next "ding" to announce his response. We usually went back and forth like this for two hours until it was time for me to prepare the kid's dinner. After a few weeks of flirting, Pete disclosed that he was a famous pop musician. My reaction was, "No way, prove it." That's when our message writing progressed to phone conversations (FaceTime wasn't available yet). When we first spoke, Pete's British accent gave me butterflies and the giddiness of falling in love. The moment that he sang his number one hit, I chose him as the perfect person to tryst with. The instant gratification side of Sharon swiftly decided on meeting him in Las Vegas. Pete thought about it for all of two seconds before coming up with a tale to tell his wife. Despite having permission, I lied to Ed that I was traveling with friends. I could've told him the truth since I already had his blessing,

Sixty-ninth Street Suicide

but I didn't want to hurt him. I still can't decide if being with another man was considered cheating even though I'd received the go-ahead. If it was the other way around, there's no way in hell I would've said yes. But I considered this the perfect opportunity for me to have a fling before settling back into married life. Once again, I was wrong.

Seated in my I-refuse-to-sit-anywhere-but-an-aisle-seat, I was too excited to concentrate on the thriller that I'd purchased at the airport gift shop. Instead, I quelled my nerves by listening to Springsteen on my iPod while constantly straightening out the nonexistent wrinkles on my linen dress. Normally I wore comfy clothes while traveling. But Pete was meeting me at the airport, and my goal was to immediately make him melt. After washing up in the ladies room upon arrival, I brushed my hair, added a touch of red lip gloss, checked out my outfit in the bathroom's full-length mirror and internally gave myself a thumbs up. Standing in the baggage area with my little black carry-on case by my side, I spent the next ten minutes studying the face of every man who passed by. As I began inching toward the huge, lit up flight arrival board, a tap on the shoulder made me stop. Spinning around, I found myself face-to-face with a man who looked like an older version of Pete. He'd sent me pictures of his younger self, but there was still an undeniable attraction. We stared at each other for a few seconds before his sexy British accent broke the awkward silence, "I was over there waiting for you, doll." He then guided me to the limo that he'd hired to drive us to the Venetian hotel.

Within minutes of entering the suite, our clothing was scattered everywhere. After fourteen years with Ed, it felt strange being with another man. We couldn't keep our hands off each other, and the sexual experience was beyond anything that I'd imagined it would be. The following morning, I was on my own. Pete was used to sleeping in until noon—as musicians do. But I'm a morning person, and my body was still running on eastern standard time. So, I set off to the hotel's shops in search of clothing that didn't fall off my much smaller frame. I'd been a size eight since forever. But as I tried on pants, even the size fours hung off my hips. Becoming and remaining slim with no effort was, by far, the best part of my journey. Later on, we strolled around Vegas and ate dinner at the hotel's four-star restaurant. It wasn't what I'd call romantic or one hundred percent comfortable since this was new territory for me. To be blunt, I flew thousands of miles to have sex with a complete stranger, and that part of the trip was a complete success. Pete and I hooked up one more time when I drove to his gig in Philadelphia. After that, we parted ways because the distance was too big of an obstacle to continue our dalliance.

Returning home from a weekend of nonstop lust didn't satisfy my so-called midlife crisis. In fact, it did just the opposite. So, I took advantage of Ed's permission to fool around and went wild. Back in New York, I experienced what my therapist referred to as manic episodes. After only being with Ed for fourteen years, the sex floodgates opened. While I'm not manic depressive, I acted out with men rather than deal with the realization that there was more to my meltdown than needing to have an affair. Some of my dates turned into one-night stands. Since I've always been a sexual person, it didn't bother me if the guy disappeared after an evening of fun. Most of the men were at least ten years younger than me. When I asked what they saw in a woman my age, they explained, "You know who you, are and you're not inhibited in bed." At forty-two-years old, it took a while before I could get used to being called an *older* woman. But I figured that being labeled a MILF was much better than feeling invisible.

John

When I think about positive dating experiences, many men come to mind. But there are two people who stand out because our relationships were based on a strong emotional connection.

John answered my eBay ad a couple of weeks before I asked Ed for the divorce. The last thing I anticipated was meeting a guy who was physically my type, smart and available. But as I drove up to his job site, I couldn't stop staring at the not-so-tall, dark and handsome man who was waving to me. When he complimented the vintage coat that I was wearing with a flirty grin, I could detect a mutual attraction butterflies vibe. Initially, it was all business as we went through the items that John wanted to consign. I don't remember how, but our conversation then somehow pivoted to our personal lives. After only a few minutes, I blurted out, "I think I need to get divorced." My subconscious was finally informing my brain what was going on inside my head. His expression said, "It's okay, you can talk to me about it." John put his arms around my waist to warm me up before asking, "It's cold. Why don't we go grab a bite to eat and thaw out?" Of course, I said yes to the man who was sending my pheromones into a tizzy. We drove together in his car and parked on a side street afterward to make out. In my mind, I'd already anointed him the future boyfriend who'd ensure that I wouldn't die alone after my divorce. I could contact John anytime, day or night, knowing he'd answer my call. He became a great source of comfort, especially after Ed and I separated a couple of weeks later. Having someone neutral to talk to was like having a therapist with benefits on speed dial.

Everything was going well until four months later when I had a psychic intuition. The feeling I got was like when someone pops into your head and you pick up the phone because you're thinking, "Oh, I should call them." Seemingly out of nowhere, I felt compelled to google John and his dog's name. Since he had a common surname, I figured that adding his dog's name would help narrow down the options. When a book fitting my key words popped up, I assumed that it was another John because this experience was feeling bizarre—even for someone psychic like me. I only had to read one page to know that it was written by my John. For the rest of the day, I barely moved from the computer, intensely taking in every word. Within hours I knew all about John's life, including the extreme abuse that he'd endured as a child. He'd never shared that part of himself with me, and I completely understood why because some of the stories in his book made me sick. But now I knew that he limped because his mother wouldn't let him see a doctor after he broke a bone while playing baseball. The scar across the bridge of his nose wasn't from a fight—unless you call your mother pounding on your face a fight. The abuse became so bad that John ended up sleeping in a car for three years when he was in middle school and too young to be on his own. This would become a huge secret if I kept it to myself. If I didn't tell John, it would be the ultimate deception and betrayal. His initial reaction was disbelief as he screamed, "How did you find it? You expect me to believe that you somehow just stumbled onto my book? I didn't even realize that it's still on the Internet." My answer was, "There's no other way I could've found it. I swear, I'm psychic and there's a reason someone sent me to read it." Now that I knew all John's darkest secrets, he felt too vulnerable and stopped contacting me. I understood why he disappeared, so I did what I needed to do—I let him go.

Derek

My most noteworthy experience was with Derek, my high school sweetheart. To this day, I still sometimes wonder, "what if?"

Derek moved from Canada to New City, New York, when we were both in the eleventh grade. He stood out from the usual suburban boys as he glided down the hall with unlaced work boots that extended his already long legs and accentuated his cute round butt. I blushed every time he walked past my locker, which was five rows down from his. It wasn't uncommon for one of us to catch the other stealing a sideways glance. I never considered myself particularly attractive, even though I had my share of suitors. So, when Derek asked me out, I was ecstatic. But I was also nervous because at seventeen, having sex scared the hell out of me. What if Derek didn't think that I was good in bed, or if he got grossed out by the cellulite on my butt? While my pheromones screamed to go for it, my inner voice played the role of a chastity belt. When Derek misconstrued my distancing as disinterest, we silently went our separate ways without breaking up or gaining closure.

Fast forward to late 2005, when part of my journey included reconnecting with people from the past. As my therapist explained,

"Reaching out to friends you've lost touch with is completely normal because you're trying to go back to a time when you considered yourself happy. So, you equate these people with happiness." Upon coming across Derek's name on classmates.com, my fingers excitedly tapped a short message on the computer keyboard; "Hey Derek, remember me? I've always wondered what happened to you after high school and wanted to say hello." Since I didn't expect him to respond, I wasn't disappointed when I didn't initially hear from him. Later, I learned that Derek didn't immediately read my message because it was sent to an email address that he rarely used. When he sent me a note a couple of months later, his bold response, "Remember you? Every detail," confirmed in no uncertain terms that my unresolved feelings weren't one-sided. When I reached out to Derek, there was no ulterior motive, and I never anticipated how one innocent message would change three people's lives. By the time that Derek responded in April, Ed and I had already separated. A minuscule amount of optimism whispered that perhaps I was supposed to be with him and live ecstatically ever after. But my demons laughed in my face. I didn't deserve anything good and definitely not something as perfect as spending the rest of my life with my soul mate. We immediately began corresponding every day. Not even one thousand miles or his marriage could stand in the way of our intense, long-distance emotional affair. Before addressing the unhappy situation with his wife, Derek wanted to meet up and see how our chemistry played out in person. I'd found the strength to ask for a divorce and assumed that Derek would too.

I'll never forget June 26, 2006. That's the day when Ed moved into his new house, which was conveniently located one block away from the family home. It was one of the last steps before we could separately move on with our lives. I knew that this would be one of the most difficult milestones of our divorce, and I desperately needed a distraction. Since Derek often traveled to Manhattan for business, I invited him to meet me in the city. What could've been a day from hell became two of the most electrifying days of my life. A rush of thoughts entered my mind upon seeing Derek stroll through the Hilton's oversized revolving glass doors. I'm sure that I wasn't the only woman who immediately noticed his tall stature, graying hair at the temples, and those same long legs that made me want to jump him. When he started moving past my table, I teased, "Hey, don't you recognize me?" We stared at each other in awe when our mutual connection was immediate and undeniable.

I tried being as respectable as possible to Derek's wife and avoided temptation by sleeping in the second room of his hotel suite. But before the sun announced a new day, I tiptoed into his room and silently slipped into his long, warm and welcoming arms. We lay like that for a long time without uttering a word for fear of disturbing this utterly blissful moment. The world froze as happiness and contentment hugged me for the first time since forever and silenced my demons. I pushed aside the challenge of our living in two separate countries and envisioned creating a life together. I'm unable to recall what we talked about at dinner that first night or when we stole our first kiss, but I wish I could. I do know that it was a great conversation because I recall floating on happiness as I fell asleep. After a cozy breakfast in the hotel lounge the following morning, we spent a dreamy day together strolling through Central Park. The air was crisp for June, and I remember thinking that this was the type of connection I'd been longing for. As we wandered from the Boat House to the Great Lawn, our lips were locked together practically the entire time. Damn, he was a great kisser, and I never wanted to stop. We were the lovebirds I'd always envied seeing around Manhattan, holding hands and acting ridiculously happy. We stopped for dinner at one of my favorite steak houses, where the meat could tempt the strictest vegan. Since neither one of us had a big appetite, we decided to split a sixteen-ounce medium-rare Porterhouse steak. After the meal was served, we discovered that while I like the crispy ends, Derek preferred the soft middle. We laughed upon realizing that even our eating preferences complemented each other. While walking off our meal on the way back to the hotel, I broached the subject of continuing our relationship. That's when Derek confided that he cared about me, but he needed to make sure that this feeling was real before he broke up his family. I was foolishly convinced that my new life would include this man, who I could undoubtedly spend forever with.

The following morning, I felt hope and happiness as we held each other close while kissing goodbye. This wasn't the end; it was just the beginning. Or so I thought. Being naïve or perhaps blinded by excitement, Derek and I assumed that we'd somehow make our relationship work—despite adding young children living in two different countries to the mix. He sent a plane ticket for us to rendezvous a few weeks later in Montreal, where he'd be traveling for business. Going from the darkest hole to the highest high felt unreal. Derek's call a week later to cancel our trip confirmed that it was. When his wife noticed that he was acting strange, she rifled through his computer and discovered our messages. After a few heart-wrenching months, I broke off all painful contact to offer Derek and his wife a chance to reconcile. I also needed time to heal and hopefully stop obsessing about this man who I adored. Losing Derek was par for the course since the story of my life was now titled, "I'll live and die alone."

My Confidantes

As my recurring nightmare of getting divorced and being alone threatened to come true, my depression seemed to hold me under water. When it did allow me to come up for air, I could only catch shallow breaths before my head was shoved down even deeper.

While I didn't have the strength to face my decision, there was no delaying the inevitable. I was down another ten pounds, and a belt wouldn't hold up the pants that I'd purchased after losing the first twenty pounds. This was also a time when my tears ran uncontrollably like a broken faucet. More than one acquaintance in town commented, "I didn't recognize you—you look completely different. Do you have cancer?" My body was drastically thinner, and my chest had all but disappeared, but to me, the mirror just reflected a thinner Sharon. I didn't hold anything back as I responded, "No, I'm not sick. I'm depressed because I think I need a divorce." I was startled when more than one woman confided, "I wish I had the nerve to divorce my husband." People who I barely knew felt comfortable opening up to me. My obvious vulnerability must've incentivized them to be honest. As sadness slowly broke my spirit, I protected myself by hiding out in the house. There was no denying that I was severely depressed. But no one knew the first thing about how to deal with my physical and emotional transformation. Especially not me.

My best friend, Sharon, was my greatest supporter. But her life was consumed with autistic twins who had two very different sets of needs. I felt guilty burdening her with my problems because, on the surface, my life was far more stable and less chaotic than hers. Despite lacking control over my depression, I still blamed myself for being sad. I knew that I couldn't just get over it, but I thought that I should so that friends didn't have to deal with what I perceived as whining. If Sharon missed my daily call, or detected a lack of energy in my voice, she knew how to cheer me up. All she had to say was, "I'm taking a trip to Macy's to return sneakers because Matt's feet are so damn wide" (Matt was her son) or "Wanna take a ride with me to Costco?" My excitement was palpable—especially since these mini bonding trips helped add a tiny bit of sunshine to my endless, raging storm.

There were four other people who I felt completely comfortable opening up to. Perhaps it was because I knew that they'd never judge me. My hip eighty-six-year-old Nana and I had the same *speak our mind* and *tell it like it is* attitude. We identified with each other's raw honesty, which created an unbreakable bond of immediate identification and empathy. She was one of the first people I told about needing a divorce and wisely advised, "Life is short. If you're not happy, you do what you have to do." When I took the kids to visit her in Florida, her eyes opened wide while critically looking me up and down. After pursing her thin lips disapprovingly, Nana threw us in her beige Cadillac to grab dinner at her favorite deli. I knew that she meant business when

I saw the speedometer creep past forty-five mph in a thirty-mph zone. You'd think that we were Hollywood royalty given the way that she introduced me and the kids to the regulars. Nana only stopped staring reproachfully after witnessing me consume a decent sized meal and my favorite chocolate chip cake with icing for dessert.

My second confidante was Lisa, who made it a point of regularly checking on me. We had a very honest relationship from day one, so it felt natural asking her for advice. When I began shedding the weight, I explained that it was due to a midlife crisis. But when I realized that the problem was needing a divorce, she initially became pissed. She couldn't understand how I didn't know what was going on in my own head and was convinced that I'd been deceitful. I'm not sure how I was so detached, either. But regardless, Lisa was my greatest sounding board and offered the wisest advice, like telling me to speak to a therapist before doing anything that I might regret.

Leslie and Andrea—my two high school friends—were my greatest supporters. They called to check in on me every day for an entire year. Half the time, I'd say, "I'm fine, but I don't want to talk." They took no for an answer and gave me my space. We celebrated birthdays together, spent a fun weekend in the city and shared many long conversations. I can never thank them enough for being true friends to the core.

The Breakup

There's no telling how someone will react until they're immersed in the situation. The angrier that Ed grew, the deeper guilt held me captive. We were caught in a wave that kept dragging us under as we fed off each other's misery.

Once, when Ed didn't agree with how I'd handled a situation, he spat at my feet before storming out of the house. His message was loud and clear—he didn't understand what was going on and had finally reached his breaking point. While walking in a restaurant parking lot one Saturday night with Lisa and Robert, Ed unnecessarily pushed me to walk faster. Lisa witnessed his outburst and became upset by his somewhat aggressive behavior. I'd transformed my easygoing husband into a vile enemy.

I had my eureka moment on New Year's Eve as we were welcoming in 2006. We'd made plans to pick up friends in Brooklyn and celebrate in the city. Morgan was sleeping at Sharon's house. Myles would stay at our friend's house until we dropped them off while simultaneously picking him up. In my rigid mind, the plan was convoluted. And leaving my comfort zone had me picking my finger for days beforehand. But expecting Ed to sit home wasn't fair, so I tried pushing myself. On our way to drop off Morgan, a fast and unexpected snow squall hit. While making a right turn onto Sharon's street, the car skidded sideways, came to rest on the wrong side of the road and miraculously missed a massive oak tree by inches. After confirming that the kids were okay, I yelled, "That's it. I'm not risking our lives to keep inconvenient plans." Through gritted teeth, Ed hissed, "I'm going with or without you." Relieved to have an out, I slammed the car door when we reached Sharon's and marched into the house with Morgan and Myles tailing closely behind. Twenty baffled expressions, including Sharon's, silently questioned, "Why are you here? You're supposed to be with Ed." Myles didn't want to stay in Brooklyn and looked as relieved as I felt. When I later overheard a friend telling Sharon that my marriage was over, I was tempted to butt into the conversation and confirm that she was right.

A week later, on January ninth, it was our thirteenth wedding anniversary. I really can't remember how or if we celebrated. Ed leaned over on the actual morning to kiss me. Wanting nothing to do with him, I snapped my head back to avoid this rare attempt at affection. His painful response will forever reverberate in my ears, "This is the most loveless anniversary I've ever had." He was right, and I knew that this would be our last one together as husband and wife. That afternoon, my next-door neighbor Jackie recommended that I call her social worker to talk things out. I desperately needed to speak with someone, so I booked an appointment with Mickey for over the Martin Luther King holiday weekend. It was during that session when I finally grasped what I needed to do and when. My plan was to ask Ed for a divorce in five months when the kids returned to sleepaway camp. Mickey responded, "If you think you can wait that long, that's fine. But you're in an awfully bad place, and we need to figure out a strategy to help you now." Ed was always convinced that Mickey talked me into leaving him, but the decision was all mine. No one tells me what to do, especially concerning something as serious as a divorce. After the appointment, I called my friend Andrea, who had gone through a similar situation. She encouraged me, "Sha, do you think you can really wait five months without totally losing it? I've been where you are, and the sooner you do it, the better." She was right. Feeling too emotionally fragile to wait even one more day, I was determined to have *the dreaded talk* upon Ed's return home from Myles' soccer game.

A half-hour later, a surreal feeling took hold as I spoke the word *divorce* out loud. "I know you've seen me falling apart, and you keep asking why. Here's what's been going on. I haven't been happy for a while, and I can't stay married to you anymore. I need a divorce." Not knowing how to articulate the emptiness I felt, I kept repeating, "There's a hole in my heart, and you can't fill it." It was the first and only time that I saw Ed cry as he pleaded, "You want to tear our little family apart?" Ed wanted to stay together. But if he'd focused on how horrible our dynamic had become, I think it might've been easier for him to digest what I was saying. What hurt the most was seeing him in so much emotional pain. I'll never understand why he wanted to stay together when you had to look really hard to find whatever respect still existed in our relationship. Many people asked why I took the divorce so hard when I *wanted* it. The divorce was *necessary*—not something I ever *wanted* to do. It wasn't like I woke up one day and said, "You know what, I think I'll tear my family apart today and screw with everyone's head." I promised Ed that he'd thank me one day for giving him this second chance at lifelong happiness. I'm still waiting for that thank you now that he's with a more suitable match.

Ed immediately began seeing a marriage counselor and begged, "Please come with me to talk to Gloria. We can't just throw our marriage away." We attended one session together, and I scheduled one appointment with her alone. But speaking with Gloria felt more painful than breaking up the family. I immediately felt disdain for her, probably because she continually sided with Ed and reminded me of an old-fashioned schoolmarm. During our one-on-one session, I shared things that I wouldn't say in front of Ed for fear of hurting him. I made it clear that since there was zero chemistry between us, the only obvious solution was divorce. When Gloria concluded that there was no way to fix our issues, she promised to help me end the marriage. But during our next couple's session, she continued to focus on patching things up. Her betrayal stirred up a rage that incited me to curse her out before insulting her by yelling, "That's it, I'm done. But don't worry, you'll still get your money during Ed's appointments." I then stomped out of her office for the last time.

There was one area where Gloria's expertise and advice came in handy. It didn't take a genius to see that I was not in a good place. The stress caused by sleeping in the same bed as Ed was an added burden. When I pointed out, "I need to have the bedroom to myself. I can't sleep with Ed there," Gloria agreed and instructed Ed, "It would be good for you to move to another room and give Sharon her space." When he asked, "Why should I have to leave our bedroom?" Gloria replied, "Sharon is obviously not faring very well. It's best to keep her in her environment where she's most comfortable." Right before Ed packed up his stuff and moved into the basement, we all sat around in a semicircle at the top of the stairs to apprise the kids of the situation. When we explained that mommy and daddy were having issues getting along, I defiantly stated, "We are not staying together." Ed, on the other hand, confidently reassured them, "Maybe mommy and daddy will work it out." It's no wonder that Myles' nine-year-old brain didn't properly process everything. A couple of days later, Morgan asked Myles, "You know mommy and daddy are getting divorced, right?" After

Myles nodded, Morgan continued, "Do you know what a divorce is?" When he shook his head with a blank stare, we were forced to relive the most heartbreaking conversation all over again.

Little things said and done often left the biggest impression. I always referred to Ed as "honey." When Myles heard me call him by his name for the first time, he sobbed, "Don't call Daddy that." It's amazing how children pick up on the subtlest things. I was able to relax a bit when Ed moved downstairs. Sleeping on my own with Trixie by my side meant that I could actually relax, get some rest and temporarily escape my demons. But upon hearing the garage door open around seven o'clock every weeknight, I wanted to stick my head in the sand like an ostrich and make this horrible situation disappear. The kids took turns sleeping with Ed because they felt that it was their responsibility to protect him. My therapist friend assured me that this was completely normal. It helped alleviate my guilt knowing that Ed wasn't alone while banished to the basement. I often wished that we could somehow skip over these painful steps and quickly come out the other side—legally divorced, living apart and moving on.

Since I was still one thought away from completely losing it, I knew that I wouldn't last another week without seeking help. When I began attending private one-on-one sessions with a recommended psychiatrist in town, he took one look at me and urged, "You need to pick up the prescriptions I'm calling in, immediately." Two weeks later, the gray cloud that I literally saw hanging over my head vanished. I was the tiniest bit better, but meds alone weren't the answer.

The greatest outcome of therapy was dealing with and letting go of my rage. For years, I was afraid of getting help because if therapy didn't work, I was doomed. But since I'd already lost my marriage, I was no longer terrified of failure. Looking back, my outward rage had turned inward in the form of a deep-seated depression. But it was a lot easier dealing with hating and berating myself than taking out my anger on my beautiful children. During therapy, I took complete responsibility for tearing the family apart and concluded that

Ed was somehow a saint. But he disrespected me in front of the kids, never showed me affection and belittled my budding career because my paycheck could never compare to his. In retrospect, we both contributed to the demise of our marriage, and playing the blame game was futile. My weekly psychiatric appointments lasted for a few months until the day my shrink sat back, dramatically crossed his long legs and with a smug look announced, "I don't think you should be getting divorced." A lot of people didn't understand how I could split up with someone I still loved. Glaring at him, I argued, "You obviously haven't been listening to a fucking word I've said." When I slammed the door behind me, I abandoned my only source of help. This spontaneous, ill-advised decision brought me one step closer to suicide.

Dear Diary

Soon after my separation, a friend suggested that I keep some sort of journal. Since sharing my thoughts seemed therapeutic, I started a public online diary at deardiary.com. It's ironic that I couldn't share my true feelings with those closest to me while strangers knew all my secrets—with the exception of my suicidal thoughts.

The first few entries discussed losing my identity when I stopped being a wife. While nothing could take away my title of mom, I'd left the workforce and no longer belonged to a family unit. Ed's house was less strict than mine with practically no rules. When I went to pick up or see the kids, it wasn't unusual to trip over five-day-old pizza boxes in the hallway. Even more disgusting was the dirty underwear that I could count on being thrown all over the kids' rooms. In addition to enjoying complete freedom, the kids avoided me and my sadness. This was one of the issues that contributed most to my feelings of worthlessness. Only through tenacity did I find the strength to reinvent myself during a time when I barely had the energy to breathe.

My first entry was written about a month after asking Ed for a divorce:

Sixty-ninth Street Suicide

Mid-Life Crisis

Posted by Sharon on 25th February 2006

I am 42 years old, married for 13 years with two beautiful kids and an adorable dog. I thought I was happy. I mean, I have the Type-A husband who gave me the million-dollar house and anything else I wanted to go along with it. And so, for 13 years, I convinced myself that it was okay to compromise. It was okay if I didn't feel passionate toward my husband. It was okay if he was more like a friend and we were living parallel lives. Well guess what folks, it wasn't okay. It's not okay.

My kids went to sleepaway camp for the first time last June. It was just me and my husband. Oh, and of course, my dog Trixie. I took a step back and saw that this was not the man I wanted to spend the rest of my life with. He is a wonderful man, don't get me wrong. He is intelligent beyond belief, kind and we have a lot in common.

But my heart had what I call "a hole in it." It still does. At first, I called the confusion inside of me a midlife crisis. I started to lose weight. A lot of weight. I am down to a size 2. Not that I was big to begin with, but I am tiny now. I still don't have an appetite, but hopefully the meds will kick in soon. Oh, but wait, I am getting ahead of myself. Forget the meds part for now. I was convinced that I just needed to have an affair to eliminate this restlessness inside of me. Hey, lots of people have affairs and remain married, right? Well, actually it is mostly men who can sleep with someone else and stay married. And I did have an affair—with my husband's blessing. And that people is a story in itself because it was with someone famous. Let's just say that I met someone online who lives in California, and I flew to Las Vegas to be with him. That was the beginning of the end of my marriage.

When I began checking out of curiosity how many people had read my diary, I was shocked to see the numbers practically double daily. At the end of the year, my diary was listed as one of the ten most popular for 2006—which I attribute to its timely subject matter. This was well before Instagram, where people can have a million followers for lip-synching while wearing nothing but a towel and holding a fake microphone purchased at Walmart. I was the woman warrior who had the chutzpah to walk away from a damn good life. Given some of the comments that I read, many women were utterly miserable. But they didn't have the strength or the guts to ask for a divorce. Some women couldn't financially afford to leave their husbands. The majority didn't want to break up their family. But the most popular reason for staying was the fear of the unknown. At the time, I didn't consider asking for a divorce as a strong or courageous act. But I now realize that I can be badass and face the most distressing situations head-on—I'll deal with the consequences later. Writing one of the most popular diaries made me feel like I had a following. Not wanting to let anyone down, I wrote about being hopeful when I was going on a date or about starting what I labeled *part two* of my life. It was mostly bullshit because, in my heart, I knew that my story was never going to end the way that I wanted it to. And it never did. As I remained single during what felt like forever, I eventually lost the motivation to continue writing. I struggled to end on a positive note, so my last entry was a lie because there wasn't any hope. Depression had convinced me that my path in life was now full of potholes, detours and an endless number of dead ends.

Wish
Posted by Sharon on 26th March 2009

> I realize that a lot of people have read this diary. I figure that most are women and a lot are unhappy in their marriage. So I really wish that I could update this with some good news on the "man" front. I can't. The last guy I dated was not over his ex, and I was not going to be the woman he used to get

over her. But I really miss the companionship that only two lovers can share. I've set my standards high, and I'm not going to lower them.

My ex has been with his girlfriend for over a year. They spend a lot of time together, and I am so jealous of them. I'm not jealous that she is with him. I envy that he has the relationship I would give almost anything for. I have begun crying myself to sleep again, but I don't think I will fall back into a depression where I am unable to function or stop crying. I put on a good mask when I go outside. I don't think people have any idea how miserable and lonely I am right now.

But again, I have to say that I made the right decision by getting divorced. Every time I see Ed now, we're friends. It's good.

I'm lucky in that I have money and don't have to worry about finances. And given the fact that I barely left the house this winter and don't eat much, I really don't need a lot of money to live on. I'm not giving up. And I hope anyone reading this doesn't either!

Remember, divorce is an ending and also a beginning. Unfortunately, sometimes the new beginning takes a while. I've waited this long. I can wait a bit longer.

Happy Spring.

Chapter 11

Family Matters

One of my greatest fears was passing down depression to my kids. It's amazing how whatever I dread always seems to come true while my wishes continually elude me.

Myles was nine years old when Ed and I split, and his young mind didn't completely absorb the situation. While I'm grateful that our divorce was amicable, I didn't know that continuing to attend events together as a family confused him. But when Ed introduced Pam to the kids six months after they met, Myles seemed to take their relationship in his stride. We didn't know that he took our rapport as a sign of eventual reconciliation until a complete meltdown. The day that I took away his Xbox when he refused to finish his homework, a festering rage revealed his turmoil. During the argument, I shut off Myles' video game while he was in the middle of a crucial battle—winning would move him up to the next level. I couldn't care less, but Myles was acting as if this was a dire situation. Suddenly he jumped up, grabbed a serrated knife that was on his desk from dinner the night before and held it two inches away from my neck. He looked like Norman Bates in *Psycho*. Shocked by this unexpected turn of events, I reactively screamed, "If you want me to die, there's no reason to live. Go ahead and kill me." As I moved toward Myles, he immediately threw down the knife—he was seemingly petrified of accidentally stabbing me. I knew that he wouldn't hurt me, but I also wasn't afraid because dying was the only way to end my pain. This incomprehensible experience probably traumatized me more than Myles because I was only staying alive for the kids. His actions confirmed that I'd screwed up his life, and it was better if I disappeared. After the incident, we shared a good cry together before I promised, "I'll get you the help you need, I'm here for you." Momma bear always had his back, and even depression couldn't crush that strength in me.

Since Myles didn't have an ounce of aggression in his prepubescent body, I assumed that his acting out came from pent-up frustration or anger. He obviously needed to talk out his issues with a professional, but Ed disagreed. As usual, he dismissed my story as an overreaction and abruptly hung up the phone after giving me a jab, "He wasn't really going to hurt you." Myles was back to his usual calm self the next day at school. Ed took this as affirmation that everything was fine. But I was the person Myles felt most comfortable venting to, and he only exposed his most vulnerable side to me. While Ed misinterpreted most of my observations as exaggerations, I was proven right about ninety-eight percent of the time. A phone call from Myles' Spanish teacher a few weeks later backed up my conviction that something was wrong. Mrs. Lindoro explained that no matter where she sat Myles in class, he couldn't focus. When he spent thirty minutes staring out the window, transfixed on two squirrels chasing each other, she suspected he might have ADD. As soon as I repeated what Myles' teacher said with a bit of *I told you so*, Ed agreed to send him to therapy. I'm still not sure how Dr. Slater gets his young patients to open up, but after only one session, Myles seemed more relaxed. Perhaps he was relieved that I'd reached out to him when he didn't have the wherewithal to reach out to either me or Ed.

I was floored by Dr. Slater's diagnosis. Myles did have ADD, but he was predominantly suffering from depression. I never recognized that his anger came from a place of sorrow because it wasn't in the same form as mine. He was sad to lose our family unit and angry that he'd interpreted Ed's new relationship with Pam as replacing me. Guilt tore me up as I blamed myself for causing his issues. God forbid if he ended up miserable like me. The next time I saw Myles, he mentioned that he wasn't eating much because he didn't have an appetite. I understood why but I still annoyed him by pleading, "Come on, you hardly ate. Just take one more bite." I hated when people got on my case about eating, so I should've known better. Eventually, I realized that he'd start eating again when he was ready. With the help of therapy and medication, Myles gained the clarity that he needed to fight off his demons. I knew that he was feeling better when he described polishing off half a pizza for lunch.

Morgan

Morgan also struggled. At the age of three, her nonstop screaming at night could be mistaken for a raccoon being beaten with a golf club.

When we were unable to calm her, she was sent to her room to get whatever was bothering her out of her system. Handling the situation this way successfully enabled Morgan to alleviate an anxiety that was unrecognized at the time. As she grew older, she never shared her all-consuming OCD or her tremendous discomfort in social settings. Since I can't rest easy unless all the labels in the kitchen cabinet are facing forward, I didn't think anything of Morgan closing her closet door at a certain angle before bed or predictably calling us to pick her up five minutes after dropping her off at a party. She also practiced food rituals, which were a secret between her and her demons—she was damn good at hiding things. Morgan dealt with the stress of the divorce by closet eating, which led to a significant weight gain. But I didn't dare say a word for fear of causing an eating disorder. Instead, I made an emergency appointment with one of the best adolescent psychiatrists in Westchester. Dr. Schippa happened to have a cancellation for the following afternoon and afterward advised me, "You brought her in just in time. She was well on her way to developing some type of disorder." Sending Morgan to therapy was an unexpected blessing. At age thirteen, she was diagnosed with OCD and anxiety, which explained a lot of her chaotic and unpredictable behavior. Since I never realized how emotionally tortured she was, I'd generalized her acting out as being a difficult child. As usual, I punished myself because I somehow should've known that Morgan's mind was running at one hundred miles an hour.

Morgan is my mini-me. So, when she witnessed my plummeting weight, isolation and crying more often than a newborn, she was terrified that the same thing could happen to her. When she wasn't going for my jugular, she revealed her resentment by saying cruel things like, "No one wants to be around you. You don't even leave the house." I understood the dynamics taking place, and I didn't blame her for not wanting her life to mimic mine because I didn't either.

After news spread about the divorce, our family became the topic of conversation around our somewhat small, gossipy town. The remark that sticks with me the most is when an acquaintance approached me to announce, "You know, Morgan has gained a lot of weight." I wanted to respond, "I know. I'm depressed, not blind."

Stressed Out, Acting Out and Freaking Out

When I recall how wound up Ed and I were, I'm amazed that we somehow dealt with everything like two adults. Sadness replaced the anger that we began harboring toward one another and helped us mend our friendship fairly quickly.

Ed insisted that he wasn't stressed out after our separation in 2006, but his actions proved otherwise. Soon after driving out of the garage with the car door open and smashing his window, he hit a tree after falling asleep at the wheel and totaled the car he'd just spent five thousand dollars fixing. I told him, "I've already traumatized the kids by telling them we're getting divorced. I'm not going to devastate them again by having to announce that Daddy is dead." He knew that I was right and agreed to be more careful. But Ed wasn't the only one who was forced to deal with his fair share of negative energy. My crappy luck helped the traffic police reach their quota for the year. The first ticket that I received was for using the phone while driving. I tried explaining to the officer, "This is an important call from my surgeon, I had to answer it. I'd just had surgery, and I'm having complications." Even after pointing to the white cast up to my left knee, he insisted on writing me up. He couldn't resist adding a speech about the dangers of talking on the phone while driving. A few weeks later, I tried shaving five minutes off my ride by taking a short cut, which entailed making an illegal left-hand turn. The cop stopped the person in front of me, talked to him for a minute and waved him off. When he then motioned for me to pull over, I complained that he couldn't pick and choose who he ticketed. But I guess that he could because I received a $150 ticket and two points off my license.

From the day that my dad taught me how to drive, he called me Lead Foot. So, the two speeding tickets that I received weren't completely out of the norm. One ticket was for going forty mph in a thirty-mph zone. A few months later, Ed and I were driving back from Myles' camp when I was stopped for going ninety in a sixty-mph zone. Ed joked, "You should try getting out of the ticket by offering the cop a blow job." He'd never been crass with me before, and it left me feeling unsettled. If I hadn't fought the second ticket, I would've had eleven points on my license. Fortunately, I hired one of the top lawyers in Westchester so that my current license didn't become as worthless as my old, expired ones. Sharon was with me when I received my last ticket for not wearing a seatbelt. I told the cop, "What can I say, it's obvious that I'm not wearing a seatbelt, so write me up." Sharon looked at me and said, "You really weren't kidding when you said that you're having a run of bad luck."

Risk but Not Much Reward

Our first notable change as a newly separated couple occurred when it was time to take the kids to California during their February break. There was no way in hell that I was going to take an awkward family trip right after our separation. We agreed that it would be best if Ed took the kids away while I stayed home and tried to relax. But spending a week alone with my thoughts was as terrifying a prospect as pretending to be one big happy family on vacation.

Desperation compelled me to write to a friend of a friend on Facebook and invite myself to visit him in St. Martin. When Paul responded yes, I found myself furiously packing within an hour for the next day's early morning flight. I never gave traveling outside of the United States and spending time with a complete stranger a second thought. My friends all agreed, "You're crazy. You have no idea who this guy is. What happens if he's dangerous and you're outside of the country?" But I wasn't scared—it's freeing to live without fearing death. I arrived in the early afternoon and met Paul at my hotel. We sat by the pool while getting to know each other before digging into a scrumptious lobster dinner. Paul worked the following day while I spent a lot of time reading a book in my hotel room. Even on a tranquil island with perfect, non-humid weather, loneliness was my one true companion. Traveling without my family was a new experience, and being on an exotic island without them was almost as bad as isolating at home. The trip began on a positive note when Paul drove me all around the island and treated me to another dinner at a local watering hole. But I couldn't get away fast enough upon discovering that he was a drug dealer.

If Morgan told me that she was leaving the United States to spend a weekend with a strange man, I'd burn her passport. But during this time, I wasn't thinking rationally and craved validation as a desirable woman and human being. It didn't work because men were using me the same way that I was using them—only for different reasons.

Splitting Up, Splitting the Assets

Upon the family's return home from California, Ed sat me down and asked one last time, "Is there any chance for reconciliation?" Avoiding all eye contact, I inspected a tiny stain on my white shirt while whispering, "No." After acknowledging that I wasn't going to change my mind, Ed said, "If you're not going to work on our marriage, let's get this over with." We were now hell-bent on splitting up the marital assets and finalizing our divorce ASAP. I'm pretty sure that our lawyers, Catherine and Neil, had never worked with a more amicable couple. When I congratulated Ed with a big hug after overhearing him mention his promotion, both lawyers questioned us with puzzled looks, "Are you sure you want to get divorced?" I'll always love Ed, but we no longer made each other happy. And we both deserved a partner who brought out the best in each other.

While splitting up the marital assets was fair and uneventful, an amusing conversation added levity to what could've been an entirely solemn situation. Decades before meeting Ed, my mom advised me and my sister, "You need to stash away some of your money in a knipple. If something happens, you should never be forced to depend on a man." A knipple is a Yiddish word that translates to a woman's secret pile of money so that she has the power to make her own decisions. This old-fashioned Jewish concept arose before women were common in the workforce. But my sister and I still heeded my mom's advice and put away money in a special savings account. Not wanting to keep any secrets from Ed, I told him about my stash early on in our marriage. During negotiations, I pointed out, "My account was saved pre-marriage to protect myself in case of an emergency. If a divorce isn't knipple-worthy, I don't know what is." Ed's Jewish lawyer immediately understood my request and said, "Oh yes, I agree. That's Sharon's money, and she should keep it." My Irish lawyer, on the other hand, asked in a perplexed tone, "What the heck is a knipple?" In the end, it remained all mine.

For me, the marriage was officially over before its legal dissolution when I noticed Ed's naked ring finger. From the day that I asked for the divorce, I'd placed my rings in a safe place—never to be worn by me again. They were now being held for Myles' future wife. But Ed wore his ring for another month while hoping for a reconciliation. Removing his simple thin gold band represented the symbolic demise of our marriage, especially since he hadn't taken it off since our wedding day. I first noticed this new development when we were all gathered at my sister's house to celebrate Morgan's birthday. Alyce couldn't understand why I was inconsolable about the missing ring and dismissed my tirade as an overreaction. But losing the one you love, even when it's for all the right reasons, is heart-wrenching. She passed judgment by declaring, "You wanted the divorce, so why are you making such a big deal out of it?" For the tenth time, I tried explaining. "I didn't want the divorce. I needed the divorce. There's a difference." Most people didn't understand my many contradictions, and they often made me feel like I was living in my own little bubble with made-up rules. But I'd understand why someone else in my situation would be upset. Why didn't Alyce see that by removing his wedding band for the first time in thirteen years, Ed was adding an exclamation point to my statement that, "I need a divorce." My sister tried being supportive all throughout my depression, and in many ways she was. But she thought that I should just snap out of it. She wanted to be a close-knit family and couldn't understand why I wasn't making an effort to spend time with her. I tried explaining that it wasn't personal, but nothing got through to her until I said something brutally honest. "Why don't you stop being overweight?" became her aha moment when she realized that depression was out of my control the same way that food had practically ruled her life.

P.S. Being Thin Didn't Solve My Problems

When my eating disorder took hold in high school, I was convinced that happiness correlated with the number on the scale. But my most challenging times occurred when I was at my thinnest weight. So much for that theory.

A huge plus with the divorce was getting the flat stomach that I'd always wanted. But while I loved being small, the rest of my life was one big shit show, and becoming thin didn't help one bit. Not being able to eat or having to worry about my weight for the first time in twenty-two years gave my obsession with food a rest. Snacking on my cherished M&Ms throughout the day is the only reason why I didn't shrink to a skeleton. I wasn't trying to lose weight, but the lump in my throat prevented me from eating, and I shed the pounds as easily as a snake sheds its skin. Whenever my underfed stomach began rumbling, I shoved down just enough food to shut it up. A few women in town seemed jealous and remarked, "You'll definitely gain it back." Here I was, a former shell of myself, and their greatest concern was my losing the weight that they wanted to lose. It was interesting to see people's reactions to my physical transformation—I was either pitied or envied.

While I was happy being thin, being thin didn't make me happy.

Chapter 12

Going from Worse to Worse

Suicide was on my mind every day to the point of obsession.

Waking up pissed me off because it meant that I wasn't dead. I was careless when crossing the street because I couldn't care less about getting hit by a car or, even better, a bus. Mind you, this was in New York City where I had a decent chance of getting plowed into by a driver who was more focused on texting than driving. I contemplated jumping in front of a subway train, but my mind could never get my body to do it. Whenever I read about someone else who'd successfully killed themselves, I was compelled to reread the article two or three times. To this day, I google the person who died because I have an odd curiosity about the life they left behind. I also fantasized about being diagnosed with cancer and not telling anyone or seeking treatment. That way, my death would be considered a natural act of nature. Imagine my disappointment when a technician saw something on my mammogram that later turned out to be benign. During the Ebola crisis, I envisioned letting the disease take its course after catching it on the subway. But internally bleeding to death seemed as horrible a fate as dropping fourteen floors from my apartment window to my death.

After one of my ankle surgeries, I knowingly walked around for a week with a DVT blood clot while praying that it traveled to my lungs. I was forced to seek treatment when it began moving up my thigh and became too excruciatingly painful to ignore. I thought, "With my luck, I'll lose my leg but survive." The night before I went to the hospital, I was with Ed and Myles in Westchester to deal with a family matter. As I clumsily fell into the car with my bright pink cast, the seam on the edge of the leather seat hit a sensitive spot. Ed must've seen me wince and asked what was wrong. Nonchalantly, I responded, "I know I have a blood clot. I just know it." Ed slowly glanced over and said, "Really?" I detected a bit of a tone that whispered, *There's always something wrong with you. What's your problem?* Whether Ed's tone was real or imagined, I felt shame about something that I had no control over.

As I lay in the emergency room the following night while inspecting the hospital's grimy, once white ceiling, I texted the kids to share my latest ailment. Morgan immediately replied, "I'm sorry, feel better, mom." Myles failed to respond, which hurt me. When I later questioned why he didn't answer my text, he replied, "My phone's broken, I didn't receive your message." That was probably the truth, but during this time, my demons were in complete control of my self-hatred and lack of confidence. They insinuated that he didn't answer because he couldn't care less about me, and I believed them. When the doctor came back to read the results, he was shocked that I'd waited a week to seek treatment. "This could've traveled to your lungs and easily killed you," he commented while shaking his head. I thought to myself, *That was the plan.* Because I had a blood clot, I was no longer medically cleared to take birth control pills, which I was using to help lessen my migraines. When I abruptly stopped, I quickly packed on three pounds. Despite being the same size and not looking any different, I became obsessed and hopped on the scale an additional two times a day. Being a victim to the numbers for so long, it took a couple of years to accept that my aging body wanted to hang onto those extra pounds.

The treatment for a DVT is blood thinners. Now that I was instructed to take it for at least three months, my blood levels needed to be checked every other week. But I didn't bother because if my blood became too thin or too thick and killed me, I'd finally die without looking like it was by my own hand.

A Heart-Rendering Move

After Ed settled into his new house, the family home taunted me with memories of animated holiday dinners, milestones like Myles taking his first steps and laughter ringing from the kid's playdates. Two years later, I sold the house to downsize, save money and have a fresh start. This wasn't an easy decision, given the infinite amount of joy our beautiful house once brought.

Cleaning out forty-five hundred square feet by myself took off another two pounds and made me pick my finger raw. But suffering was a much better option than burdening anyone by asking for help. Going through my long-deceased father's papers from eleven years earlier and reading my cheating fiancé's cards espousing his undying love added sorrow and anger to the depression. To make matters worse, New York was experiencing heavy rain showers practically every night that summer, and the basement window had a leak. With so much rain pouring in like a waterfall, it took me a good hour to wipe up the concrete floor. Since the house was on the market, it was imperative that I hide this imperfection. An obvious leak and a damp basement weren't exactly selling points for prospective buyers. Whenever the clapping thunder sent me scrambling to the basement, I locked Trixie in my bedroom before flinging my body down the stairs to experience my nightly hell. I consoled myself that once the move was over, I'd start a new life where happiness was on my side.

Everything about moving was emotionally draining. Panic set in when I learned that my rental house wouldn't be ready on time. I immediately concluded that camping out in Ed's basement was the best solution. He responded yes, probably in part because he'd witnessed me becoming frailer by the day. The fact is that he never stopped caring about me, even though I was convinced that he felt nothing for me but disgust. Staying at his house was doubly awkward since he was already engaged and living part-time there with Pam. Hiding downstairs and entering and leaving the house from the back entrance was cringeworthy. I berated myself for getting into such an uncomfortable situation, especially when Ed entertained *our* friends upstairs. As if things couldn't get any worse, Trixie refused to stay with me in the basement. She somehow sensed that people at the top only slept upstairs. Since I was at the bottom of the pecking order, even my dog wanted to have nothing to do with me.

A Doggone Traumatic Goodbye

Upon finally settling into my new rental a week later, Trixie kept me company whenever the kids were at school or staying with Ed. Having someone around who unconditionally loved me made my isolation the tiniest bit more bearable.

We'd raised Trixie from a seven-week-old tiny timid ball of black and brown fur into a stubborn, feisty and loyal member of the family. But after the divorce, she quickly transformed from a source of comfort into a subject of concern. Trixie didn't like sharing my attention with other females, and Morgan was her biggest target. My Wheaton Terrier had turned into what I now called my Wheaton Terror, and she was putting my daughter in harm's way. It took a lot of emotional strength to give Trixie away, but in my mind, this was another punishment. While I was looking for a nice family to adopt her, I came upon a Facebook dog rescue group. They put me in touch with a lovely older couple who wanted a senior dog like Trixie. When I told Trixie's future mother that I'd drop her off after the Jewish holidays, she adorably called to her husband, "Marvin, Trixie is Jewish." Upon announcing that I'd found Trixie a new home, Ed remarked, "You're never going to give her away, you love her too much." Out of my mouth flew a response that sums up the strength I've acquired during my journey. "If I can ask the father of my children for a divorce, I can give away my dog."

On Trixie's last morning home, Myles bawled while tightly hugging her furry neck for one last time. Relief was written all over Morgan's face, and I don't remember her saying goodbye to our once calm member of the family. An hour later, Trixie was restlessly walking around in circles on the front leather passenger seat of my Infiniti SUV during what felt like a never-ending drive to Connecticut. Her restlessness annoyed me until I reminded myself that this little baby didn't have a clue that she was about to be abandoned by the only mother she'd ever known. The road became blurry as tears rolled down my face and dampened the thick collar of my black velvet coat. I was done with having to be so brave and strong.

Upon driving up the bumpy pebble-filled driveway to Trixie's new home, Evelyn greeted us on the porch with a wave and a friendly hello. Inside her quaint, tidy house, we talked about Trixie as she checked out her new environment by copping a sniff here and there. Evelyn gently scolded her not to jump on the furniture and pointed to a greenhouse-like room where she said, "Trixie will be sleeping there." This added tremendous guilt because I knew that Trixie would be miserable with this new arrangement. She was used to not only sleeping with me but sleeping on me. After about twenty minutes, I began sobbing. Evelyn kindly urged, "You should probably leave now, it'll make things easier for the both of you." With the heaviest of hearts, I climbed back into my car and quickly drove away. The last image of my fur baby was her stubby wagging tail as she followed Evelyn into her new home. She erroneously thought that I'd be back soon to pick her up. I added this experience to my list of why I wasn't worthy of breathing the same air as the rest of the world.

Myles' Surgery

Myles was born with a beauty mark on his left tear duct. As he grew bigger, so did the mark. I decided to have it removed before it became a complicated surgery and left a bigger scar. Since it was sitting on such a delicate spot, a pediatric plastic surgeon was chosen for the job.

Yom Kippur seemed like a convenient time to book the surgery since Myles wouldn't miss school. But I didn't realize that Ed was identifying more with his Jewish identity and planned on spending the day in temple. When I told him about the appointment, he declared, "Don't expect me to be there. It's your fault for making it on a religious holiday." When my sister also announced that she couldn't come because she'd be in temple, I should've changed the date. But I was too caught up in my paranoia to take a step back and properly assess the situation. I took Ed's anger as a personal affront and decided that he could no longer stand being in the same room as me. After reevaluating Ed's reaction in a more rational light following my suicide attempt, I see that he had every right to be pissed off about my poor timing. It had nothing to do with me personally.

Myles awoke from the anesthesia with a massive headache that initially concerned the doctor. This was his first experience being put under, and watching him scream when he wasn't throwing up rattled me. The only solution was letting him rest while hoping that the headache would subside. I must've had a pathetic look on my face because the nurse came over to comfort both of us before Myles finally drifted off to sleep.

Legally Divorced, Officially Single

I constantly picked my finger while anticipating the legal dissolution of our marriage. We'd signed the divorce papers over the summer. But there was no date set for their arrival because they had to go through the court system. Not knowing when our divorce would be official meant that I couldn't immediately gain closure.

Ed's painful gaffe didn't help matters. In New York State, getting divorced within the first year of a legal separation requires that the dissolution be based on abandonment. Ed and I agreed to wait so that our once beautiful relationship didn't end on such an ugly note. But for some unknown reason, Ed's lawyer took it upon himself to write up the divorce papers early and based it on abandonment. It contained disgusting language like my withholding sexual relations for at least one year, which wasn't even true. After receiving the papers, I called Ed hysterically crying while screeching, "You got me back. We're even." Ed had no idea what I was talking about until we deciphered that he'd authorized the legal paperwork without first bothering to read it. Knowing how quickly he went through the mail with the concentration of someone with untreated ADD, I realized that it was an innocent mistake. I then promptly tore up the papers in my attempt to symbolically erase this painful incident.

When the divorce papers arrived months later, I practically held my breath as I grabbed them from the courier. But a wave of peace washed over me upon removing them from the thick, oversized manilla envelope. The court date stamped on the papers was our wedding anniversary, which meant we'd gone full circle. I considered this a definite sign that the divorce was the right move since I don't believe in coincidences.

Physically Falling Apart

While lying on the cold metal operating table, I casually informed the anesthesiologist, "Don't feel bad if I die, I don't mind." Everyone in the room gasped in unison, "Don't say something like that." But I meant every word.

My first ripped ankle tendon opened the door to three additional operations on my left ankle. When one tendon went two rounds of surgery without success, I told the doctor, "I don't want it. Please replace it with a cadaver tendon." My health had become so pathetic that I now required the help of a dead person. After another surgery, I awoke to throbbing pain in my left eye. I asked a nurse, "Why does my eye hurt? The doctor operated on my ankle. At least I hope he did." She hesitantly informed me that the anesthesiologist accidentally scratched my cornea while taping my eyes shut. I later learned that this was a rare, but common mistake. But in my mind, it happened because I deserved to suffer. An ophthalmologist was called to put in eye drops before taping a patch over my eye, making me look like a pirate. Being forced to hobble on crutches with limited eyesight was additional confirmation that the sun was never going to shine brightly for me ever again. Friends accused me of being a hypochondriac, but doctors don't operate on healthy people. My response was always, "I'm not a hypochondriac, the doctor always finds something wrong. What I am is pathetic."

Simple activities like bringing a cup of tea to my room required an exhausting slide upstairs on my butt and a half-hour nap afterward. Not wanting to inconvenience the kids, I only accepted help when they offered it, which was almost never. I surmised that they were desensitized after seeing me have an operation on a yearly basis. But as they grew older, their indifference contributed to my perceived irrelevance because they didn't care enough to help the mom who never failed to support and protect them. If it was Ed who needed help, I was convinced they'd remain by his side 24/7. Each grueling surgery added to my conviction that the kids wouldn't miss me when I finally overdosed.

Poor Timing

When a sudden illness ruined the most exciting plans that I'd had in months, it fed my negativity more than any surgery could.

After my mom called to announce her annual trip to New York, I jotted down with excitement the week that she and her boyfriend Stanley would be in town. I then organized a fun day shopping at our favorite outlets. As usual, we had to eat lunch at the diner where my mom relished the granola like a connoisseur savors a rare wine. Spending cherished time with family gave me something to look forward to, and I excitedly counted down the days like a child anticipating Christmas. Upon laying down to sleep the night before, pain similar to labor sent me racing to the bathroom. Doubled over in waves of agony, I threw off my clothing as sweat dripped profusely from every pore and diarrhea endlessly flowed. I remained in the bathroom until 3:00 a.m. before crawling into bed and catching a couple of hours of unsatisfactory sleep. By the following morning, the intense pain had abated to a really bad stomach ache. After using the bathroom for the first time in daylight, I realized that my so-called diarrhea was actually blood. The scale

Sixty-ninth Street Suicide

was down three pounds and confirmed that I was dehydrated and very sick. Taking a deep breath, I called my doctor friend Larry who said, "Calm down, I'll meet you at the hospital in a half hour with my associate, who's an excellent gastroenterologist." Larry was a friend I could always rely on to be there. Despite having many good friends in my life, I always thought that no one liked me because I hated myself. After my examination confirmed that I was still bleeding, Larry and the gastroenterologist immediately began filling out admittance papers.

Despite feeling like I'd just given birth, I was convinced that I'd go home and spend time with my mom and Stan. Instead, they were forced to visit me at the hospital while I silently cursed my body for turning against me. Only a loser would become hospitalized during the one week of the year when their mom was in town. The following morning, a colonoscopy revealed that the culprit was infectious colitis, typically brought on by stress. It's commonly found in people who suffer from depression because our repressed emotional pain often presents as physical ailments. Upon discharge, I drove myself home and resumed my solitary life with nothing to do and no one to hang out with. My mom and Stan were spending the day with my niece and nephew before flying back home the following morning. While calling to say goodbye, I was glad to hear that she ate her favorite granola for breakfast and bought three bags to take home.

Another Hospital Visit

I found myself back at my old stomping grounds—the hospital—a couple of years later, when I suspected that a stabbing pain on my right side was appendicitis. Larry suggested calling Sharon to take me to the hospital, but it was late. Even though she was the most generous person I've ever known, inconveniencing my best friend in the wee hours of the morning was not happening.

While lying alone in the emergency room with my eyes fixed on the slowly dripping IV, Sharon suddenly poked her head in before entering the room with her signature grin. "Why didn't you call me? You shouldn't be here by yourself?" Larry had called her against my wishes. It's impossible to articulate the pure joy mixed with utter guilt that simultaneously washed over me. We spent the next half hour laughing about how I should either move into the hospital or marry a doctor. Sharon wouldn't leave until a scan revealed that a burst ovarian cyst was the source of my discomfort. I'll never forget her love and support, and I can still envision how she lit up the room with her love and kindness. While I was able to do things alone, it was a nice change of pace when I didn't have to.

RSVP: No

Sharon was one of the only people who could coax me to go somewhere because our indescribable bond fed a small part of my broken soul. One day she encouraged me, "Why don't you come with me to volunteer at the school store? It'll get you out of the house for a couple of hours."

Third graders marched across the gym in perfect formation with dollars and coins stuffed into their tightly squeezed fists. They were as excited about buying stickers and pencils as I am when purchasing anything from Chanel. Myles ran over to give me a bear hug while his teacher admonished the rest of the class to remain in line. An hour later, uncontrollable tears forced me to hide in the corner. Sharon kindly walked me to my car and said, "Hey, I'm proud of you for trying." But I focused on the negative and my failure to keep it together for two measly hours. It shouldn't be that hard.

The thought of attending any kind of social event put me in a panic. In an attempt to stop feeling guilty whenever I was put in the position of saying *no*, I asked friends to exclude me from parties and special events. Tina didn't invite me to her son's bar mitzvah. Penny didn't extend an invitation to her anniversary party because she knew that I'd be doubly uncomfortable by not knowing anyone there. It was a relief that even if some people didn't understand depression, they recognized that I was going through a rough patch and honored my wishes.

My close friend Leslie from high school called to ask, "Are you going to our thirtieth high school reunion? It'll be fun to see what everyone looks like now." Seeing old friends did sound like fun. But the thought of making small talk with people I hadn't seen in years seemed as terrifying as speaking in front of a thousand strangers. Instead, I sat home that night, cursing myself out for not going and imagining all the fun I was missing. During the few times that I did muster the courage to get out of the house, leaving early was my M-O. I'm not sure what was worse—not trying or giving up. But as my therapist says, "I can't change the past, so I need to stay in the present to become emotionally healthy for the future."

If ending depression was as simple as trying to feel positive or looking on the bright side, there would be less or possibly no suicide. And if it was a physical ailment like cancer, instead of a mental disability, more people would stop dismissing it as merely feeling blue. When you think about it, no one in their right mind would give up ten years of happiness to plan the perfect suicide.

Chapter 13

Two Deaths and One Survival

By the winter of 2010, I'd had enough; it was time to end the pain. While spending another solitary Saturday night watching TV, it felt like someone suddenly grabbed my arm and pulled me to the medicine cabinet. Without hesitation, I swallowed my last ten Ambien pills and then went to sleep convinced and excited that I wouldn't wake up.

Since I'd once blacked out after taking one Ambien pill, I surmised that a few were enough to kill me. Surprise, surprise, taking ten pills is not a serious suicide attempt and won't kill most people. It had taken me four years to summon up the nerve to kill myself, and I couldn't even do that right. I noted that during my next attempt, more pills would be needed. The day after gulping down the Ambien, my head wouldn't stop spinning. But otherwise, I was fine. Morgan noticed me walking around like a drunk and asked, "What the hell are you on?" This wasn't a cry for help, and I wouldn't ruin my next chance to overdose by confessing the truth. After suffering from major depression for so long, I was convinced that no one wanted to hear me go on about something that I should just get over. So, I kept the pain to myself and descended deeper and deeper into my perpetual dark cave at the bottom of the ocean.

*I knew that I was depressed. But I thought that I was a loser, and that's why I was depressed. In reality, I thought that I was a loser **because** I was depressed.*

There was nowhere to turn because I was meant to live an unfulfilling existence and suffer eternal punishment for the abortion. My shrink said that most depressed people tend to share this distorted way of thinking. Looking back with a clear head instead of being in my head, nothing at that time made sense. Experiencing happy moments meant that I was OK because depressed people were sad every second of their life. At least that's what I once thought. Plus, I stopped losing weight, and my crying spells were shaved in half. It didn't occur to me that isolating in the house for days or weeks on end and constantly obsessing about suicide were as dangerous to my mental health as shooting up meth every day.

Nana

When my mom planned a big shindig in Florida for Nana's ninetieth birthday, everyone was on my case when I refused to go. Walking to the mailbox was a challenge at this point, but I was expected to fly alone to Florida and stay in a hotel room by myself. The thought of sleeping alone was as depressing as going to a couple's dance and being the only one without a partner.

Missing Nana's birthday celebration sits near the top of my list of regrets. Most of the immediate family flew down for her special day. But when her closest grandchild didn't show up, she was devastated. I didn't have the emotional strength to go, but trying to explain that to my mom and sister was like talking to someone who didn't speak my language. This wasn't my choice, depression was running the show, and I was its puppet.

But when I received my mom's frantic call a year later, stuttering between sobs that Nana was on her deathbed, even a category five hurricane couldn't have stopped me from flying down. I was initially confused because when Nana had called me the night before, she sounded perfectly fine. While interrogating Mom, I asked, "How can she suddenly be in a coma when she was okay last night?" Upon receiving an evasive answer, I knew that my mom was hiding something.

Like me, she sucks at lying. It was now even more imperative that I get to Florida, see Nana before she died and uncover the truth. After frantically booking a flight while simultaneously packing, I asked Ed for a ride to the airport. Perhaps I shouldn't have, but his refusal to take a forty-minute ride when I was fighting against the clock really stung—especially since he knew how much I adored my Nana. I then made plans with my sister, who suggested, "Park your car at my house, and I'll drive you to the airport. It's only ten minutes from here." Not thinking clearly at the time, I never considered calling a car service.

Within hours, I was leaning over Nana's hospital bed, stroking her crepey soft arm while willing her closed eyes to look at me for one last time. I whispered, "I'm so sorry I wasn't there for your ninetieth birthday. But you know I love you with all my heart and I'll see you again soon. Tell grandpa I say hello." Kissing her luxuriously silky cheek, I tearfully smiled knowing that she'd passed down the family's unusually soft baby skin to me. I then turned to Mom and insisted that she tell me what the hell happened. All she said was, "Nana took some pills. She couldn't stand the pain from her spinal stenosis any longer." I tried stopping the conversation by saying, "Okay, I understand. I don't need any more details." But Mom being Mom, she continued explaining that Nana had finally reached her breaking point and ingested all the Ambien in her medicine cabinet. I considered this a courageous act and was beyond jealous that she'd found the nerve to overdose while I hadn't—yet.

My mom further explained that before this time, Nana had instructed her husband Ruby not to call the paramedics if he ever found her sick and dying. But when he discovered that Nana was unconscious, he panicked and did exactly what Nana told him not to do. Fortunately, either Ruby didn't read Nana's suicide note, or he forgot to mention the overdose to the doctors. Otherwise, they might have pumped her stomach and possibly saved her. If she'd survived, they also would've had to revive Ruby because Nana would've done everything possible to kill him.

As I stood over her, Nana suddenly opened her eyes. When she saw my face, she wagged her finger in my direction. I interpreted this as one of two questions: "Why are you here?" was directed toward me. "Why am I alive?" was meant for Ruby. One minute later, she closed her eyes for what would be the last time before she passed two days later. This was a situation where I desperately missed having someone close to support me. I wanted to send a text message saying, "I arrived safely, and I'm with Nana now." I'm pretty sure that I texted Alyce. But she and Nana had a complicated relationship, so she lacked the empathy that I needed. My kids understood, but the last thing I wanted to do was burden them.

With Nana and I both wanting to die, but for very different reasons, death became a reoccurring theme of our phone conversations. While her mind was youthful and sharp at the age of ninety-one, her brittle, permanently hunched-over back tormented her day and night. Like most of the women in our family, an acute allergy to pain pills prevented her from obtaining relief. We often discussed her less-than-stellar quality of life and how we couldn't understand the thinking behind people who wanted to live to be one hundred. She confided in me that she'd considered taking pills. But when her neighbor across the hall overdosed, the poor woman survived as a vegetable after her roommate found her just in time. She also considered driving her car into a wall, but neither one of us was sure that she could follow through. We both cynically laughed when I joked, "With your luck, you'll somehow survive and live out the rest of your life without legs." They were morbid but somehow light conversations. This was the closest that I ever came to outing myself.

The night before her overdose, Nana gifted me with one last phone call on my landline. Normally, I would've ignored the ringing phone on my way out, but something or someone compelled me to answer. Little did I know that this would be the last time that I'd hear the high-pitched, nasally Brooklyn accent that would've made a great cartoon character. We had a regular conversation about what I was up to before ending the call with our usual, "I love you." If she'd confided in me, I never would've tried talking her out of suicide. My focus would've been on telling her not only that I loved her, but all the reasons why.

What I loved the most about Nana was her sense of humor that came out even when she wasn't trying to be funny. One of the many hysterical memories that stands out is when my uncle, aunt, Mom, me and the kids went to a nice dinner on the water to celebrate Morgan's birthday. When Nana told us that we were leaving at four o'clock, we knew not to question her even though the reservation was for five o'clock. As a result, we made the Early Bird Special even earlier that day by arriving thirty minutes before the restaurant officially opened. When we arrived at four-thirty, the staff sat us down immediately. But they definitely didn't seem thrilled. Right after the appetizers were served, no one came back to ask if we needed anything. We couldn't catch anyone's attention because the staff was huddled in a corner, seemingly having a meeting. Nana then proceeded to shout, "Fire." After the waiter and two other people came running over, Nana asked, "Could we have some more napkins and a fork, please?" Morgan and I laughed about it for years.

When I asked Mom and Alyce a few months later if Nana had called them the night of her overdose, their answer *no* startled me. I'm honored that she gave her middle grandchild a special thought, forgave me for missing her party and blessed me with the gift of one last conversation until we meet again.

Morty

Death was one of the only times that I could be counted on to leave my comfort zone without hesitation. In addition to Nana, I had the honor of supporting my mother-in-law, Lenore, when her husband died. Morty was sixty-four when his fading memory began interfering with his legal career. Once every test conceivable ruled out all other illnesses, the diagnosis was Alzheimer's disease. Ed and I were still together at the beginning of his affliction, and watching this once vibrant man regress to a child was a journey I hope to never take again.

Alzheimer's provided a glimpse of how cruel life can be. One time when Ed left the room, Morty animatedly remarked, "I don't know who that man is, but I really like him." It was one of the saddest things that I've ever witnessed. At dessert another night, Morty grabbed a newly opened ice cream container from the table. He appeared as delighted as a two-year-old as he dug into his favorite flavor straight from the carton. Lenore kindly chastised him. But the kids and I laughed because he looked so damn pleased with himself. He sat quietly at Myles' bar mitzvah and commented at the end of the service, "Wow, I really enjoyed that." Alzheimer's patients retain their oldest memories the longest, so it's likely that the service reminded him of going to temple as a child. The only positive thing about Morty's illness was that he never knew that Ed and I had been divorced.

In August of 2010, Morty was admitted to the hospital a few days before Ed and his family left for their annual summer vacation. Lenore had gone to the bathroom for all of one minute when Morty became dizzy, hit his head on the sharp end of the dresser and required stitches. Unbeknownst to Ed, Morty's health began deteriorating the day before his trip. Perhaps Lenore was in denial, but for whatever reason, she didn't give anyone a heads up. Morty died at almost the exact moment Ed's eight-hour car ride to Maine with four young hyper kids came to an end. When he called me with the news, I didn't hesitate rushing to the hospital to support Lenore and kiss Morty goodbye. My father-in-law was a smart, successful attorney who'd become a coveted father figure after my dad died. When the company where I was working went out of business, Morty asked, "Do you need a hug, little girl?" He already knew the answer as I immediately snuggled into his long welcoming outstretched arms. Divorcing Ed didn't mean that I stopped caring about my in-laws. Upon arrival at the hospital, Morty looked like he was sleeping. The crisp white hospital sheet was tucked under his chin, and he wore a peaceful expression that I hadn't seen in years. My warm tears ran down his cooling, leathery skin as I kissed him on the forehead and thanked him for taking such good care of me. It was nice spending time alone with Lenore and feeling needed instead of judged.

Upon his return from Maine, Ed helped Lenore with the funeral arrangements. The burial site was chosen years earlier, so it was just a matter of putting the plans in motion. When I inquired about finding a ride to the funeral, Ed said something along the lines of, "My car is full, go ask someone else," before taking off and leaving me to fend for myself. This made me feel like a piece of crap and reinforced that I no longer belonged. At the service, I distanced myself from everyone else because my sick mind told me that I was no longer a part of the Greenwald family. Everyone drove back to Ed's house after the funeral. I quickly headed home after making small talk for a few minutes. Feeling awkward and shunned, I wanted to be alone to wallow in my pity. I now realize that no one had a clue how much I was suffering, or was ignoring me, either purposely or unintentionally.

An Almost Not-So-Sweet Sixteen

Ed's annual trip to Maine was a huge point of contention because it meant that I wouldn't be with Morgan on her sweet sixteen. He hadn't bothered checking with me first to see if I was okay with missing such an important milestone. I wasn't, and he probably didn't bother asking because he already knew the answer.

When I became inconsolable upon learning of his plans, I was accused of overreacting. This would've been upsetting even if I was still my gregarious, charming self. But my depression turned this difficult situation into a tragedy. In addition to Ed failing to check in with me before booking the trip, Morgan didn't seem to consider my feelings and nonchalantly advised, "It's okay, we'll celebrate when I get back." So, in my mind, Ed despised me, I was replaced by Morgan's stepmother, and the entire family couldn't care less about me. If I saw my partner unfairly excluding his ex-wife, I'd explain why it was wrong and undo the damage. Ed's solution was inviting me up to Maine to join in the celebration. If I couldn't stay alone in a hotel room for Nana's birthday, it was even less likely that I'd accept Ed's invitation to whoop it up with his new family in Maine. In my mind, Ed was trying to placate me and essentially saying, "I know you won't come up to Maine by yourself, so you can celebrate when we get back. I gave you an option. It's not my fault if you didn't accept it." However, as if the universe had other plans for me, I was with my baby on her big day.

It sounds cliché, but things really do happen for a reason. I believe Morty died on the week of Morgan's birthday because the universe agreed that I should be included in her celebration. Since Morgan's birthday was two days after the funeral, her party had turned into a solemn shiva. But I was determined to arrange something memorable to mark this milestone. Her first driving lesson was booked for the week after she was originally due home from vacation. After explaining the situation, the driving instructor assured me, "I'll pick her up tomorrow at three." Morgan screeched as the car boldly marked "Student Driver" pulled up in front of Ed's house. We all watched from the window as she skipped to the car, excitedly flapping her arms like she did as a baby. She loved the experience, and upon returning, we all sang happy birthday out of tune as she made a wish and blew out the candles on her favorite red velvet cake.

Chapter 14

From Africa to Manhattan

Morgan was preparing to leave the nest and begin her freshman year at USC. So, the beginning of 2011 was my last chance to take the kids on an unforgettable family vacation before we all went our separate ways. We agreed on an African safari, which was at the top of my bucket list.

It felt odd being in charge of such a big trip because that responsibility normally fell on Ed, but everything went smoothly, and no one got eaten by a lion. As we drove into the Serengeti, hundreds of zebras and wildebeests parted like the red sea. Absorbing the beauty of animals thriving in their natural habitat allowed me to put most of my negative thoughts on hold. But when the tour guide drove so close to a pride of lions that I could hear the male with the golden mane panting, a horrendous thought crossed my mind. Since I was standing where the truck's extra-long vertical custom window was completely open, I could jump out and experience a quick death. My next thought was imagining how the kids would react after seeing their mother become a lion's main course. Needless to say, I quickly disregarded that disturbing idea.

Around this time, Morgan and I were constantly butting heads because she was uncomfortable with my depression. Nothing I did was right; everything I said was wrong. While we only had one fight during the entire ten-day trip, it was a doozy. Morgan was in charge of taking pictures with the new camera she'd received for Chanukah. But while leaving a resort to go glamping in another part of Tanzania, she accidentally left the battery charger under the bed. Even though she took sole responsibility for the camera, and I asked ten times for everyone to check that nothing was left behind, she decided that this was somehow my fault. Since this was our only camera, except for the ones on our flip phones, there was a good chance that the battery would run out before the trip was over. After I was ripped a new one for hours, I finally lost it. We were unpacking in our glamping tent when I pointed to myself and announced, "That's it. I'm firing myself as your mother. I'm fired!" Morgan is astute, but my action must've caught her off guard because she looked like a wounded ten-year-old whose best friend just said that she didn't like her anymore. The following morning, Morgan was back to her sassy, sweet self, and I reinstated myself as her mom immediately after she apologized. Even better, the battery lasted up to the very last day.

A few months before the trip, Ed and Pam had purchased a house twenty minutes north of the family home and five minutes away from Myles' private school. Myles immediately declared, "I'm not staying with you during the week. I can sleep an hour longer at Dad's house." With that one sentence, my future would begin a lot sooner than any of us anticipated. My final move to Manhattan was based on Myles living with me part-time until 2014 when he'd enter college. Morgan was beginning her first year in California. That meant that I'd be completely on my own in the town where I raised my family, which would be extremely awkward. So, I asked Ed for his blessing to move into the city earlier than we'd discussed. Thankfully, he said yes. He'd witnessed my downfall and thought moving out of Westchester might bring me out of my funk. This wasn't an easy decision since both Myles and I viewed my moving away from him as abandonment. I became the topic of many of Pam's and Ed's arguments because she felt that Ed took on too much responsibility. When you add in the guilt of no longer seeing Myles every day, it was a decision that I hated having to make. One day when Myles refused to see his psychiatrist, I went in his place. I wanted

Dr. Slater's opinion about my moving away. I was sure that he'd agree it was selfish to leave Myles. On the contrary, he offered, "Sometimes you have to do what's healthy for you. Myles is capable of taking the train to see you, and you can drive up to see him." His reassuring words took me by surprise and helped me do what was necessary if I was going to hold onto any semblance of sanity. Since I lived on Sixty-Ninth and Third Avenue when I moved into the city upon graduation, I considered it fate finding the perfect apartment a block away on Sixty-Ninth Street and Second Avenue.

Upon arriving home from Africa, it was time to begin packing for my big move to Manhattan. I assumed that boxing everything up would be easy, especially compared to cleaning out the family home. But while emptying the outside shed, I was proven wrong. Most of my belongings were stored in plastic containers except for one cardboard box. Unbeknownst to me, a mommy mouse had decided that the box made a great nesting ground for her babies. While going through my belongings, I lifted the box flap and nearly fell on my ass. Out sprang a mother mouse who appeared as abruptly as an old-fashioned Jack-in-the-Box. She nearly became attached to my screaming face before scampering away. Then it was my turn to react. I stomped up and down like a tantruming two-year-old. When I could breathe again, I cautiously used the end of a broomstick to risk a second look. This time I was prepared for daddy mouse to come flying out like Mighty Mouse. Instead, I discovered a carefully crafted nest of golden straw-like material.

Perched on top were black somethings the size of my thumb. Upon closer examination, I discovered four babies who couldn't have been more than twenty minutes old. As a huge animal lover, this finding became torture. I was pretty sure that mommy mouse wasn't coming back after our unfortunate encounter, and these little ones were doomed to a horrible fate. My choices on humanely dealing with the situation went from bad to I can't deal with this. I could leave them in the nest to starve and die, put them in the grass where they would probably become a scavenger's lunch or starve and die, or leave them out to get picked up and crushed by the garbage truck. My choices came down to the best way to murder them. Underneath the nest in the box were all the cards that my first fiancée Steven had written to profess his undying love. Getting rid of that useless trash didn't require a second thought. I gently placed the entire box on top of the silver can at the end of the driveway. It was garbage pickup day on my side of the street, which was the only thing that went right that day. I quickly stepped away after saying that I was sorry. But it took me another day to shake off this horrific experience and return to the shed. I didn't find it funny when friends joked that I should've drowned the babies in a pail of water. This impossible situation added to my feelings of hopelessness. Not only was I a bad person, but now I could add murderer to the list.

Not Living Large in the Big Apple

I'm not sure if I was trying to run away from my problems or running toward a second chance. Either way, moving back to Manhattan delayed my inevitable suicide attempt.

Upon awakening at night to use the bathroom in my two-bedroom apartment, I often stared out of my expansive living room window. The sounds of the city—my favorite city—drew me under its spell. This was the first home that I could call my own and the beginning of a wonderful new life. Or so I thought. It was tough leaving my Westchester friends behind, and it took a while to make one or two new ones. So, most of my days were spent forlornly staring out of my living room window. When the weather cooperated, I sat on Gotham Cafe's faded wooden bench at the end of my street. I discovered that observing the neighborhood's nonstop action was a good way to pass the time. When a job eventually occupied my days, I saved people watching for weekends.

My apartment was located on the Upper East Side, where baby strollers were the most popular mode of transportation. Living in a family-oriented neighborhood where every other person was walking a dog, I felt safe and in my element. Across the street from my building was an old grocery store that looked like a popular resting spot for mice and cockroaches—I only shopped there once during a milk emergency. The run-down building stood out compared to the beautiful multimillion-dollar brownstones that ran down the rest of the street. In the middle was a prominent, old yellow church—at least one hundred years old—that rang its bell every Sunday at noon. On my side of the street were low apartment buildings that allowed the sun to warm us up in the winter and make us sweat in the summer. Tall trees lined the entire block with flower beds planted around them. Scattered throughout the Upper East Side were the usual suspects—nail salons, dry cleaners, food stores, restaurants, bars and more nail salons. Many celebrities lived nearby, and I glimpsed at least three from *Real Housewives of New York City*.

The first friend I made in the building was Caryn. I practically mowed her down when she stepped out of the elevator holding Harvey, her ten-week-old Wheaton Terrier. Caryn and I quickly became as close as sisters and hung out often despite a fifteen-year age difference. We also fought like sisters and eventually had a falling out. I made a couple of other acquaintances, but they couldn't compare to the lifelong friends I'd left behind. My negative state of mind also prevented me from making plans because seeing them through was nearly impossible. I was convinced that I didn't have a life or any friends and made it a self-fulfilling prophecy by locking myself away in my apartment.

Another way that I passed the time was with a new form of torture that I called *Studying the Facebook Pages of Presumably Happily Married Friends*. Michelle was glowing as her husband hugged her swollen pregnant belly. Nancy posted pictures of her family holding koala bears in Australia, and Sammi was surrounded by her tight group of friends in practically every photo. But it was my roommate from straight out of college whose life I coveted the most. Sara married a well-known multimillionaire and posed in picture after picture with the upper echelon of Manhattan. Seeing the lavish parties that she threw at her ten-thousand-square-foot home in the Hamptons or looking regal at her immaculately decorated brownstone in the city always worsened my already sour mood. I decided that her life was perfect until I couldn't find her husband in even one photo.

The pictures that played with my head the most were those of Ed's new family, which included my kids and excluded me. I relied on Facebook to catch up on Morgan and Myles' lives since they didn't text or call very often. Most of our get-togethers were based on celebrating holidays or birthdays. Feeling completely separated from the children added to my strong conviction that they would quickly get over my suicide.

Desperately Seeking Help

After a few months of not working or connecting with many people, I was desperate for advice. So, I made an appointment with a social worker. Marlene was a good listener, but she couldn't provide the magic solution that didn't exist.

When I received my insurance statement a couple of sessions in, I discovered that she was overcharging me. At the next appointment, I questioned, "Why are you charging me a forty-dollar copay when my insurance statement shows twenty dollars?" I was dumbfounded by her response, "I can't afford to live here on what the insurance company pays." Even my therapist was taking advantage of me, which I blamed on myself. Stunned, I wrote out a check for the full amount. Upon returning home, I cursed myself out for paying Marlene when she actually owed me money. Had I really become this pathetic? I promptly marched to the bank and put a stop on her check. Afterward, I called Marlene to give her a heads up that I canceled the check because what she did was illegal and dishonest. Her response was simultaneously shocking and hysterically funny, "Does that mean you're not coming back next week?" Exasperated I yelled, "How could I ever see you again when I don't even trust you?" She most likely would've lost her license if I'd reported her. I let it go because I didn't want the responsibility of ruining another person's life. But, I received the universe's message loud and clear. My life was never going to get better, so I might as well stop trying. Instead of searching for another therapist, my Plan B was hoarding pills.

I tried finding another way to get through each day. A local hospital's support group for depression seemed worth checking out. Meetings began with the young leader asking people around the room to share something about their lives. Every week an older gray-haired woman with a tattered pink cardigan discussed having nothing to do since retirement. I sat far away from her to avoid catching my worst nightmare, retirement loneliness. A middle-aged man, who was a head taller than everyone else, stood out like the Jolly Green Giant. Except that he was far from jolly. He always crouched in the corner to remain invisible. Despite never raising his hand, he was always called on by the group leader. I had to listen very carefully to hear his whispering voice. Learning about his past job as a museum curator was riveting. But hearing that depression had snatched his beloved career, partner and friends made me feel sorry for him. I stopped attending meetings when they began making me anxious to the point of an inflamed, rubbed finger. In my mind, I didn't fit in because I no longer looked like a character straight out of *The Walking Dead*. But in hindsight, I was probably just as broken as half the people in the group.

If I were an observant and objective reader, I'd wonder how the narrator didn't realize that she was depressed if she sought help for depression. I'll try to explain this as best as I can, especially since one of my goals is providing insight for families dealing with a loved one's mental illness. Whenever I was isolated in my apartment or someone took advantage of me, I placed the blame on myself. My life was worthless, no one loved me, and I attracted nothing but negativity. Since I believed that my depression was permanent and arose from being a failure, the only fix was death.

Back to Work

Being alone wasn't my only fear. I needed to rejoin the advertising workforce, and I wasn't sure if anyone would hire a forty-seven-year-old copywriter who lacked digital experience.

After being a stay-at-home mom for nine years and living on alimony that was about to end, it was time to create my own source of income. Many advertising creatives were forced to leave the industry during the 2008 recession. But I offered two unique advantages. After many years away, my thinking and attitude were fresh, and I was willing to accept a lower salary than my experience warranted. My brother-in-law advised me to sign up on LinkedIn as I went about my search. Soon after, I enjoyed a personal reunion while reconnecting with old colleagues I hadn't heard from in years and sometimes decades. One of them hired me for a freelance role that eventually evolved into a full-time job. Despite being depressed, my motivation and gumption never waned, and I gave 100 percent to every project. I was known as the dependable writer who could always be counted on to meet the tightest deadlines. One of the inconsistencies of my depression was how high functioning I was at work. Being responsible, regardless of anything else that was going on in my life, kept the professional part of my life compartmentalized and healthy.

 I didn't consider it strange when one day out of nowhere, Mike, the Creative Director, called me into his office. But since I'd been laid off at least three times in the fickle world of advertising, I should've known that something was up. When I saw John from HR sitting across from him, I began sobbing before anyone could utter a word. I'd heard this story before and knew all too well that its unhappy ending was unemployment. As often happens in advertising, a few of us were laid off due to unexpected budget cuts. Convinced that I'd never find another advertising job at the ripe old age of forty-eight, burning tears ran down my face and stained the front of my favorite ruffled silk blouse. News of the layoffs immediately spread from cubicle to cubicle around the office. As I walked back to my desk, one of my coworkers read my defeated body language and offered me a Valium. When it kicked in fifteen minutes later, I'd never felt so good after losing a job. I practically floated out of the office and headed home for a nice long nap after hugging everyone goodbye.

Chapter 15

The Good, The Bad and Cancer

The week before Thanksgiving, I always ordered a fourteen-pound turkey and a large juicy brisket from the kosher butcher. Ed took off work the day before to cook his scrumptious cheesecake, vegetable stuffing, onion appetizer and anything else that he felt like adding to that year's holiday menu.

Our house rang with laughter as guests began appearing midafternoon. Morgan and Myles' squeals of delight announced the arrival of grandparents bearing gifts. Without failure, I was eventually forced to defend my lack of cooking skills while everyone gushed over Ed's culinary talent. Thanksgiving was my favorite holiday until our separation in 2006. But in 2011, it went from worst-case scenario to a godsend.

I didn't have plans for my first Thanksgiving in New York City and felt uncomfortable inviting myself somewhere. That would be akin to asking for help. So, I hung out with the doorman and scarfed down a cold Food Emporium pumpkin pie straight out of the box. When Sharon heard that I'd be alone, she apologized, "I can't invite you to Cindy's house for the holiday." But being the most amazing friend, her no was quickly followed with, "Why don't you come up on Saturday, and I'll make a homemade dinner for you, Craig, Samantha and the boys?" As I strode up the stone path to her house, my senses went into overdrive smelling pumpkin pie, turkey and something else that I later learned was grandma's secret stuffing recipe (the secret was soaking the bread in bourbon).

Everyone who knew Sharon would agree that she was generous. So, it didn't come as a surprise when she served a holiday dinner that could've easily fed the entire neighborhood—twice over. Every inch of the round wood dining room table was crammed with one homemade dish after another. Sharon was worried that a fifteen-pound turkey wasn't enough for eight people, so she also served her signature meat lasagna. There were two pumpkin pies made from scratch, one of which was devoured by yours truly. Whenever I joked about the ridiculous amount of food, "Who doesn't like leftovers?" came the reply. After piling our plates high, we dug in as if this was our first meal since ending a fourteen-day juice fast. Both Craig and Sharon beamed at me after dinner like they would to a toddler who'd finished all her vegetables. They sent me on my way with a tin full of leftovers that kept me well-fed for the following three days.

The love shown that day made me feel like I mattered, like I belonged. So, when Craig and Sharon mentioned at dinner that they were buying the boys iPads, I silently decided to chip in. It took a half-hour to scrawl the perfect thank you note in legible handwriting and without any cross-outs. After getting mushy about how much I'd always cherish our friendship, I wrote out a check and rushed to the post office after placing a stamp on the envelope. No one, including me, writes handwritten notes anymore. But instinct, or perhaps intuition, led me to put my appreciation down on paper. When Sharon called a few days later to thank me, it might've been the last time that I heard her speak in her regular voice. Unbeknownst to any of us, that would be our last meal together. If I had plans for Thanksgiving, that beautiful memory wouldn't forever be ingrained in my heart.

A couple of weeks later, Sharon told me that the doctor had upped the dose on her asthma inhaler because she was having trouble breathing. When she could barely catch her breath a week later, Craig drove her to the hospital. On the way there, she called to give me a quick update. I could hear her labored breathing before putting the phone to my ear. Using all her energy, she whispered, "I can't breathe. I'm going to the hospital because I know something is wrong. I'll let you know what the doctor says. Love you." The hospital x-rays exposed a looming shadow. After running a few more tests, an endoscopy determined that she had a large, possibly cancerous stomach tumor. Upon hearing the news, Sharon's husband fainted from the devastating truth—he might be forced to live out the rest of his years without the love of his life.

My doctor friend, Larry, called me at work to provide an update on the latest findings. In a panic, he declared, "To be honest, the shadow on the x-ray looks like cancer to me." Running into an empty office, I slammed the door and stifled uncontrollable screams with the crook of my arm. This was my worst nightmare, and I didn't know who to turn to if it wasn't Sharon. After collecting my thoughts while curled up on the office's leather couch that had seen better days, I texted Morgan. Once she calmed down, I suggested that she call or text Samantha to offer support. Neither one of us realized that Samantha was still in school. Even worse, we had no way of knowing that Craig and Sharon were waiting to share the news with her in person. Larry never gave me a heads up, so Morgan texted Samantha and inadvertently gave away their secret.

Sharon could only communicate by text, but I could read the anger in her words, "Why did Morgan say anything to Samantha? I'm so upset with her." Feeling insufferable guilt, I profusely apologized and pleaded, "Please don't be mad at Morgan, it was my fault. Larry didn't tell me Sammy was still in school." How could I think rationally after finding out that my best friend might be dying? I hated myself for making such an idiotic blunder and internally cursed Larry for putting me in this awkward position. My last text message to Sharon read, "I'm so sorry. I'll leave you alone for a while and give you some space." But that promise flew out the window the following day when Larry called and, in a somber tone, announced, "The tumor has been diagnosed as stage four aggressive cancer." Feeling awkward about my honest mistake was now the least of my worries, I'd never forgive myself if I didn't steal whatever precious moments were left with my soul mate. While visiting Sharon in the hospital the following week, her nieces shot daggers at me as if I'd planned on hurting her and Samantha—for whatever reason I could never fathom. During our ten years of friendship, Sharon and I never had one argument. Craig was now responsible for giving the all-clear as I arranged hospital visits around his nieces. The doctors wanted to send Sharon to die peacefully at home. But her fighting spirit insisted on giving aggressive chemotherapy a try, and I understood why. When her mom died a few years earlier, we shared an intense conversation regarding death. Being suicidal, I wanted to die young. Sharon's response will always haunt me, "I have to live forever to take care of the boys."

Myles and I visited Sharon during her short respite at home after the chemotherapy failed. The knot in my stomach reminded me that our next visit would either be in the hospital or at her funeral. Before going to Sharon's bedroom, I paused to give Craig a bear hug and ask how he was doing. At a loss for words, he just shook his head and sighed. We found Sharon twisting this way and that on her unmade bed as she attempted to find a comfortable position for her cancer-riddled body. Her white nightgown accentuated the few dark, stubborn hairs poking out of her otherwise bald head. My heart exploded when she asked me to rub her aching back because something so intimate was only reserved for loved ones. Watching my best friend's health rapidly decline at her young age was impossible to accept, and all the more tragic because she was leaving behind autistic twins. I would've gladly traded places with her, and every day I wished with all my heart that I could. Sadness was intertwined with guilt that I didn't treasure my life while Sharon did everything humanly possible to save hers.

February 3, on Sharon's forty-ninth birthday, it looked like cancer was going to win. I stayed home the night of her birthday party because I wasn't invited, and I didn't learn about it until weeks later. When I questioned why I was excluded, Craig's weak excuse was, "We didn't want you schlepping to Westchester from the city on a Friday night." Sharon died a month later, and her last birthday party was a beautiful memory from which I was gypped. Of course, I blamed being left out on my stupid mistake, which was probably the case.

The only way to handle the pain was by avoiding it altogether...

...But on the morning of March 7, facing Sharon's death became inevitable. I was coordinating shoes with outfits before packing my black leather carry-on suitcase for Paris. Morgan had graduated high school a year early and was taking advantage of this time to study at the Sorbonne. Myles and I were going to spend time with her while celebrating my forty-ninth birthday. The plan was for Myles to meet me in the city around noon, where we'd then taxi together to JFK airport. Little did I know how drastically my plans and my life were about to change. Larry knew how frail I was and downplayed Sharon's status because he didn't want me canceling my trip. Sharon was now intubated and no longer breathing on her own, but when I asked what that meant, he brushed it off as not being a big deal. Sharon's sister-in-law, Debbie, didn't agree with Larry's coddling and called me to spell out the facts. When I asked what to do, Debbie declared, "If it was me, I wouldn't go." That was all I needed to hear. Within an hour, I let Myles and Morgan know that the trip was canceled, sobbed to Expedia about why I needed a refund on an expensive non-refundable reservation and bolted to the hospital.

Upon my arrival, my adrenaline was flowing given the abrupt switch from a birthday celebration in Paris to the death of my best friend. The situation also felt surreal since this was the same hospital where my dad had died seventeen years earlier. Walking off the elevator, I ran into a large crowd and saw some familiar faces who led me straight to Sharon's room. Feeling as awkward as a kindergartner on her first day of school, I lingered by myself right inside the doorway. To my relief, Debbie waved me over. Upon shuffling closer to the bed, I was transfixed on Sharon's pasty white face. It felt awkward that I'd only visited her twice in the last two weeks. When I asked Larry why I didn't see her more often, he suggested that I was in a bad place and couldn't deal with such a huge loss. Did I stay away from my best friend the same way that I'd protected myself from the pain of losing my dad? I'll never know because I completely blocked out that period of time—numbing my feelings had become an automatic response. Craig described Sharon as being animated and joining in the conversation earlier in the day. I'm not sure why, but most people have a burst of energy right before they die. While I was able to whisper goodbye in her ear, I'll always be painfully heartbroken not hearing it back. The only movement that Sharon made was when another one of her friends said, "Oh look, Monique is here to see you." Monique was Samantha's best friend and had formed a close relationship with Sharon while spending a lot of time at her house. Sharon used all her strength to smile, which looked more like the Joker's menacing grimace. At the time, I jealously wished that she had saved that simultaneously scary looking but beautiful smile for me.

When Samantha began crying, I hugged her and said, "Your mom *loved* you very much." Her nieces immediately shrieked, "She isn't dead yet!" I wanted to shout right back, "She'll die soon, so stop picking on me, my heart can barely breathe. I'm losing her too!" Instead, I corrected myself and said, "She really *loves* you so much." Her unforgiving family ruined my last days with Sharon. When her nieces left after visiting hours, my trembling lips whispered into Sharon's ear everything I wanted to say. "Thank you for being the most amazing friend I've ever had. I'm going to miss our phone conversations, but I promise I'll talk to you. Please leave nickels on the ground as a sign you're saying hello. I love you." Although Craig immediately forgave me, my guilt over Morgan inadvertently telling Samantha about the cancer didn't stop haunting me until I almost died. After intense therapy, I know that what's done is done, and I can't take back a mistake that happened five years ago. While mindfulness has become a chic catchphrase, living in the now has helped me let go of things that I can't redo from the past or control for the future. Craig and Samantha slept at the hospital that night. Not wanting to intrude, I waved Craig out of the room and whispered, "Do you mind if I stay?" Looking like his mind was focused on nothing and everything at the same time, he said, "Stay. It'll help if you're here to comfort Samantha."

Sharon's large private room provided more than enough space to accommodate sleeping arrangements for guests. Samantha and I slept on rolling beds like the ones that are used for donating blood and caught a few hours of restless sleep. Craig slept on the uncomfortable mushy couch in the corner. Sharon's brothers and Debbie left for rest and a refreshing hot shower before returning to the hospital the following morning. After everyone else was gone, we enjoyed much-needed comedy relief while sitting semicircle around Sharon's bed. Craig and Samantha were seated directly across from me when, in the middle of a serious conversation, Craig blurted out of nowhere, "Where are your eyebrows?" The look on his face was that of a child concentrating really hard to figure something out. Appropriate or not, we had tears running down our faces—this time for a good reason. Within months, I had my eyebrows professionally tattooed.

It was inevitable the following night that Sharon would be gone before the sunrise announced a new day. In addition to the group who slept at the hospital the night before, Debbie and Sharon's brothers remained after visiting hours. I glanced down at the warm, chubby hand that had reached out to me countless times during our ten years of friendship. Out of respect, I asked her family if they wanted to hold her hand. I was relieved when everyone shook their head. Everyone deals with death differently. While they were distancing themselves, I wanted a front-row seat to support her until her very last breath. After Craig gave the nurse permission to take out the breathing tube, Sharon's inhaling and exhaling instantly became laborious and slower. The six of us gathered around her bed, our eyes following each shallow breath that no longer filled her lungs with air. The heart that once gave her life was counting down to its demise.

After her breathing hadn't matched her heartbeat for a while, I knew that she was essentially gone. No one moved when Sharon made the death gurgle—which I believe is the soul leaving the body. It was obvious that they didn't understand she had passed, so I looked Samantha in the eye and softly whispered, "Sammy, she's gone." Samantha bolted out of her chair and wailed, "No, Mom, don't go. I love you." One of Sharon's brothers ran out of the room to grab a nurse as if this was an unexpected code blue. I'm pretty sure that the time of death was 11:14 p.m. Sharon died on March 9, 2012, while my dad died at the same hospital seventeen years earlier on March 9, 1995. When Sharon took a turn for the worse on the seventh, I knew that she was going to pass on the anniversary of his death. I sounded like a broken record telling everyone who walked into the room that Sharon was dying on the same date as my dad. Right before leaving the hospital, I tore off the March 9 page from the hospital calendar and quietly slipped it into my bag.

On the way to Sharon's funeral two days later, I found a nickel on the ground while walking to the train. My best friend was already sending me signs. Upon arrival, Sharon's family wanted items placed in the coffin. Grabbing the opportunity to kiss her goodbye, I eagerly volunteered with possibly a bit too much enthusiasm. The family handed me a couple of notes and a few pictures of Craig and the kids, her brothers and nieces and a black and white photo that might've been her parents. I had the honor of tucking the photos and notes inside of her white satin coffin while caressing her cool cheek with tears. Ed attended the funeral service. Right before leaving for the cemetery, he commented on how close I seemed to Sharon's family. It made me feel good knowing that not every family member had disowned me as an honorary member.

After my dad died, I didn't allow myself to feel the pain of losing such a significant person. Saying goodbye to my soul mate was equally upsetting, especially since this unexpected journey hadn't yet sunk in. Sharon's passing took a significant part of me with her. I was still

Sharon two, but it no longer had relevance without Sharon one. As I grow mentally stronger, I've begun making peace with my best friend's death. I'm eternally grateful for the ten amazing years that we shared together. When I describe our relationship to people, they often respond, "I've never had a friend like that, but I wish I did."

I don't necessarily believe in God, but I'm highly in tune with spirits. When my dad was gone, my greatest wish was getting one more hug. He visited my dreams a few times, but he didn't hug me until I was falling apart after the separation. I clearly remember telling him, "This feels so good. I'm never going to let you go," as my thin arms struggled to hold him firmly around his solid waist. The following morning, I eagerly called Sharon to share my experience. We often discussed how much we loved and missed our dads, and she was excited that I'd finally received my long-desired hug. Sharon obviously took my words to heart because a month after she died, she visited me in my dreams and enveloped me in a beautiful long hug. Once again, I said that I was never going to let go because it felt so good. Even in death, Sharon is always here for me and the best friend that I'll ever have.

While sitting shiva, Debbie and I discussed my Paris trip. She suggested that there was still time for me to rebook it before Myles went back to school after March break. It sounded like a great idea, so that's exactly what I did.

Chapter 16

My New Abnormal

It felt like everyone belonged to Ed's new extended family, including Pam's ex-husband, and that I was the unwelcome third wheel. If there was a photograph of everyone, I'd be the person standing on the end, easily expunged with the snip of a scissor.

Right before the wedding, Ed and Pam moved into their sprawling modern home in upper Westchester. As the oldest child, Morgan had a private room in the basement with a huge walk-in closet like you see on *The Real Housewives*. On the top floor, Myles chose the only kid's room with an attached private bath. He decorated it like a college dorm with a mini-fridge and an oversized chair for playing Xbox. The kids once again belonged to a family unit, and they quickly settled into their new normal. Ed understood that I was in a bad place, but he didn't recognize how some of his actions impacted my psyche. As a newlywed, he wanted to please his new wife—and rightly so. But it sometimes came at my expense.

After Morgan's high school graduation in 2012, Ed arranged a celebratory family lunch. It was two hours of fun and laughter as we reminisced about Morgan's shenanigans, including her hitting a mailbox with her car. She refused to take blame because, "The mailbox shouldn't have been there." I cherished these rare moments when I felt happy and included. But I also experienced an internal awkwardness because I believed that Ed only invited me out of obligation. While riding the train home from a family event, I always felt like a prisoner who looks forward to his time outside, but dreads when it's over because it means going back to solitary confinement.

The day after graduation, Morgan invited her friends to Ed's house for an end-of-school-year party. I wasn't included because Pam wasn't comfortable having me around. If Myles hadn't slipped, I might've never found out about the party. When I called Morgan to express my dismay, she dismissed it with, "It's not a big deal, we celebrated at lunch yesterday." I knew those were Ed's words, and I hated him at that moment. This blatant rejection reinforced my feelings of worthlessness and hopelessness. Facebook didn't fail to torture me. In my feed was a photo of Morgan's friends hamming it up for the camera. In another post was a table full of catered sushi with Ed's stepsons in the background. What upset me the most was a photo of Morgan grinning from ear to ear while striking her typical *hand-on-hip* pose. By the time I went to sleep, my cheeks were chafed from sobbing for hours. My misery was compounded by a blaring migraine and a picked-raw finger.

The Good Is Great

After the divorce, March 11 became a day of dread that had nothing to do with becoming a year older. But my birthday in 2013 was memorable for all the right reasons.

My good friend Caryn knew that my past birthdays were spent alone. So, she went out of her way to ensure that my fiftieth was memorable. We planned a vacation to the Cayman Islands with the same group of girls I'd traveled with to China. Upon arrival, I was hyper from anticipation, knowing that the next five days would be centered around me and my big 5-0. I was the only one at the villa who didn't share a bedroom. Caryn said, "It's Sharon's birthday, she gets her own room. Plus, she's the oldest." The girls were at least fifteen years younger than me, but my youthful personality fit right in.

My birthday was spent on a daylong boat ride with our flirty tour guide Jeff, who obviously enjoyed spending time with five attractive New Yorkers. He and I shared a dry sense of humor and one-upped each other the entire day. After sailing the calm crystal blue water for a couple of hours, Jeff suddenly stopped the boat. "Okay, guys, get ready to meet some stingrays." They were about the size of hubcaps and initially seemed daunting with faces way too small for their large round mushroom-looking bodies. But Jeff goaded and teased us until we all jumped into the invitingly clear, surprisingly warm water. When a stingray swam by and tickled my ankle, I bent down to touch him. I instantly fell in love with bodies as soft as butter and adorable big round eyes that were a bit too close together. That night, we feasted at a fancy restaurant on the water surrounded by tanks full of bizarre-looking tropical fish. Caryn ordered three birthday cakes with candles so that I could make three separate wishes. She thoughtfully remembered how important it was for me to blow out a candle and make a wish on my birthday. No one had gone out of their way to do something special for me in a long time, and I treasured every minute. At the same time, my demons taunted me to enjoy this birthday because it was a fluke. They were dead set on ensuring that it would never happen again. On the last day of our trip, my sadness returned with a vengeance. Instead of catching the last rays on the white sandy beach with the girls, I stayed in the apartment and read a book. There was no escaping my demons—I'd simply enjoyed a five-day reprieve and would soon return to my purgatory.

I also dreaded summers in Manhattan because I didn't have anyone to hang out with. To pass the time, I often jammed to Springsteen while surveying the cultural mix of tourists in Central Park. Summoning up the energy to go was a good day; most days were bad. But the summer of 2014 stands out because I accompanied my friend and neighbor Iris on day trips to the Hamptons. Iris was a celebrity photographer who shot A-list parties. While she bopped around snapping photos, I spent my time people watching. Some of my more noteworthy sightings included Christy Brinkley, Naomi Watts and the Real Housewives of pretty much every state. It felt liberating to escape my apartment for the entire day and attend events with the creme de la creme of New York. We usually returned home in the wee hours of the morning, which made my weekend feel like it was packed with excitement.

During the rest of the year, I dreaded the weekends and holidays. They were spent holed up in my apartment while trying to figure out ways to pass the hours. I must've been the only person in the entire world who asked HR, in all seriousness, for permission to sell my vacation days to coworkers. If I did arrange to hang out with someone, I'd have to follow through or become known as the friend who always canceled. And I didn't want to unfairly obligate the one or two people I perceived as merely tolerating me. When the kids were home from college, visiting them at Ed's house made me grateful for that tiny window of contentment.

When my coworkers Carolyn, Stephanie, Debra and Howard sometimes asked on Monday morning what I did over the weekend, I usually responded, "Nothing, I have no life." They thought that I was joking, but in reality, I was being brutally honest. It's probably the closest that I ever came to sharing the depths of my despair with anyone besides Nana.

Bad Dog

In 2015, I made the tough decision to rescue a dog. I'm a huge dog lover, but I was too depressed and set in my ways to care for one. Plus, being completely responsible for another soul interfered with my suicide plans. But after talking myself into something that I knew deep down wasn't a good idea, I found myself staring online at a tiny white and beige Shih Tzu rescue.

The post said that her name was Pearl, but I immediately changed it to Poppy. Dana, the rescue person in charge of shipping the dogs to New York from Puerto Rico, described her as a sweet, healthy one-to-two-year-old. But when she limped out of her crate at the airport, my eyes bulged, my heart sank, and my mind freaked out. Poppy was the exact opposite of what Dana and I expected. There were two rows of drooping nipples, exposing the fact that she'd been bred, and probably often. She was emaciated and coughed like a three-pack a day smoker. Yet, something prevented me from feeling empathy for this suffering soul. As if this nightmare couldn't get any worse, she tottered like a drunk woman in six-inch heels.

All I wanted to do was make a quick getaway, and I desperately needed advice in deciding what to do. Feeling all alone in the world, I squashed my intuition and brought Poppy home. After she kept me up the first night with her smoker's cough, Dana arranged for me to take her to the vet. While there, we added a heart murmur and collapsing trachea to Poppy's growing list of ailments. Knowing all too well what it felt like being the underdog, I wanted to give Poppy a second chance. But I never connected with her. And once I began risking the loss of a finger every time I put on her leash, giving her back was easy. Once again, something good ended in the worst possible outcome. Looking back in a healthier light, refusing to bring Poppy home would've been the obvious solution. Dana could've fostered her while searching for another family to give her the love she deserved. An emotionally healthy person would've chalked it up to experience and quickly moved on. But this situation brought me down another notch because I'd left my comfort zone by tucking away my suicidal thoughts to help another soul and fell horribly short.

A month after the Poppy incident, a couple of the girls I traveled with to the Cayman Islands were celebrating New Year's Eve in London. I originally declined their invitation because leaving Poppy so soon after her adoption didn't seem right. But now that I no longer carried that responsibility, I joined them in an attempt to start 2016 on a positive note. Any sort of positivity died when I overdosed six months later.

New Job, New Obstacles

Getting hired for a full-time job helped me deal better with my suffering. During the week, I had a place of salvation, spending quality time with coworkers, who quickly became like family. It was the only place where depression sat on the sidelines five days a week for eight glorious hours.

Despite my poor disposition, I kicked ass at work by having the confidence to take charge and the dedication to meet deadlines. The clients liked me, and the account people appreciated how much easier I made their job. Thriving at work convinced me that I wasn't depressed. Everyone was happy with my performance, except for my boss, Peter. Being the second woman in a department of fifteen creatives should've tipped me off to his misogyny. Peter would regularly shoot the breeze or complement the guys at the agency with a slap on the back and, "Great work." On the other hand, he barely said two words to me on any given day. A rare "Good morning, Sharon" would raise the alarm. "Why did he say hello to me? Is there something I don't know?"

During most of my three years at the agency, I was dedicated to keeping a client from taking their business elsewhere. Before my arrival, mistakes were made because no one had bothered getting into the headset of their complex audience. Peter trusted me and my work partner, Howard, to run the account with little supervision. At least he gave me that much credit. In the end, the client not only chose to stay at the agency but also increased their budget year after year thanks to the entire team's hard work. Many account people requested that I work on their assignments, so my boss should've been happy having me at the agency. Instead, he was either on my case or entirely ignoring me, which fueled my paranoia and put a damper on my happy place. I remained on high alert as if needing to keep an aggressive dog at arm's length or risk getting bit. My job was all that I had, so I endured the abuse in order to keep it—not having a job at all would've been much worse. I couldn't figure out why Peter treated me differently until he refused to promote Vicky—the only other woman in the creative department.

Vicky was a talented, hard worker who won the most prestigious awards for the agency. Yet, every time she asked for a promotion, Peter brushed her off with, "I'll see what I can do."

Vicky told me that her ridiculously low salary forced her to schedule quarterly meetings to repeat the same conversation that he repeatedly ignored. "I juggle these many accounts; I've achieved this and that and have earned the right to be promoted with a pay raise." When she felt like she was wasting her time during their fourth meeting, she abruptly handed Peter her resignation and essentially said, "Screw you." Here was another dedicated and responsible female who was not being shown the respect and acknowledgment that she deserved. I was proud when Vicky handed in her resignation after seeing that there was no future for her there. Ironically, my boss once told me that his wife advocates for equality in the workplace.

During my last year at the agency, I spent a good amount of time flying to financial conferences around the country. I loved traveling, getting a reprieve from my monotonous life and producing award-winning work. Hey, I was even okay sleeping alone in a hotel room. This was one of the most fulfilling phases in my career, despite my boss's bullying. But while working at a conference in Indiana, everything changed when I went head-to-head with a freelance interviewer. When I overheard Taryn telling the client that she wasn't impressed with my writing, I wanted to explode. Instead, I took a deep breath and forced my face to look calm. A colleague also described how Taryn spoke negatively about me to the client when I wasn't at dinner one night. Taryn and I were both writers, and her insecurity had apparently brought out her evil twin.

I was proud of myself for holding my temper and acting professionally, which was admittedly difficult for someone who's animated and sometimes defensive. But Peter only listened to one side of the story and decided that I was wrong before giving me a chance to defend myself. He always acted like a macho jerk whenever he heard or saw something that he didn't agree with. In fact, it wasn't unusual to hear him losing it on someone from the opposite side of the building. He wanted me gone and thought that he'd finally found a good reason to make it happen.

Right after the conference and a few months before my suicide attempt, Peter called me into the only conference room that had a solid door. Upon arrival, I saw my friend Tanya from HR and thought, "Oh shit. What is his problem now?" I was dumbfounded as he accused me of things that made zero sense and, to be blunt, were lies. He spat, "I heard you've been banned from the next client conference." Truly perplexed, I replied with a bit of a tone, "What are you talking about? I was never going to the next conference because of budget constraints." At that moment, I knew that he was speaking out of his ass. During the ten minutes that he spewed utter nonsense, all I could think was, "OMG, if I lose my job, I'm going to kill myself." When Peter concluded the meeting with, "You'll be getting a strike on your record," I was devastated by this unexpected turn of events. I didn't think that I could survive without my job. Later that day, Tanya assured me, "I saw that you had no idea what Peter was talking about. Don't worry, I'll handle this." The women in HR always had my back, which meant a lot to me.

It disgusts me to admit that after the meeting, I trod even lighter to avoid losing my job. What I wish I'd done was quit after speaking my mind. But I was a shell of my former self and didn't believe in myself enough to stand up to my boss. Work now became a new source of anxiety and my unhappy place. Peter was still hell-bent on firing me, so he decided to fabricate my review, which we discussed two weeks before my suicide attempt. To sum it up, he made me sound as competent as Steve Carell from *The Office*. Once again, HR was there to protect me because they knew what Peter was up to. Fighting for my job symbolically became fighting for my life. At the time, I didn't realize how much that thirty-minute meeting affected me. If my suicide attempt two weeks later had been successful, I'm sure Peter would've wondered if he unwittingly played a role. He definitely didn't make things easy for me and possibly accelerated my attempt. But the only thing that he was completely responsible for was unjustly kicking me while my demons were, too.

Chapter 17

Serious Suicide Risk

Being prescribed the lowest dosage of Xanax is one of the reasons that swallowing almost two hundred pills didn't work their magic. If I'd refilled just one more bottle, or added Oxycodone to the mix, I definitely would've been a successful suicide.

Every few months, I'd ask my doctor at the headache clinic, "Could you please send a refill for Xanax to the pharmacy?" Her usual response was, "Of course, but given your intolerance, I'm only prescribing .25 milligrams." A sensitivity to most pills fed my fear of throwing up during my overdose and surviving. My doctor never knew that the Xanax was solely for the purpose of killing myself. The hoarding continued until I was convinced that there were enough pills. Four clear brown Xanax bottles sat waiting in a straight line in the medicine cabinet—I was ready to go. I emotionally relied on the pills as my way out but never told a soul because there was no way in hell anyone was going to stop me. Knowing that I could end my pain as soon as I summoned up the nerve provided the wrong kind of hope, but it also quelled my anxiety.

Since I'd never kill myself without first putting my affairs in order, I drew up a will in 2012, stating that the kids would split everything fifty/fifty. Whenever they were at my apartment, I pointed out my valuable sculptures and paintings to ensure that they weren't thrown out like pieces of junk. I also constantly said the password to my safe, but repeating it back became a game since their memories were like mine after menopause. The only other subtle hint was when I asked them if my being cremated bothered them. Since I've always been comfortable talking about death, dwelling on a subject that most people consider morbid didn't seem odd. I also drew up a Living Will, and much to my sister's dismay, Ed was the primary executor while she was designated second in charge. If you want to live, you put your sister in charge. If you're intent on dying, you choose your ex-husband. After I awoke from my coma, Alyce insisted that I make her the primary executor. But I informed her, "Ed won't keep me around as a vegetable, but you, I'm not so sure."

I've often read about celebrities who go home and kill themselves, despite seeming perfectly fine hours earlier. They might be laughing with their kids or making future plans, even though their intention is going home to die. I believe their acting normal, or even happy, is sometimes because they've reached the giddy stage where they know that they're soon going to end their pain.

It's impossible to put into words how I suddenly knew that it was time to die. The decision was made in the nanosecond it takes to flip on a light switch. Never having felt this way before, it was exhilarating to finally gather the nerve that I'd waited ten years for. The plan was simple and thought out a long time ago—swallow all my hoarded Xanax pills, go to sleep and never wake up. The End. The weekend before my attempt, I didn't leave my apartment once, not even for food. Instead, I wasted another two beautiful summer days isolated like a prisoner in solitary confinement. Dreading the long upcoming July fourth holiday weekend without plans was more than I could bear. Compared to spending the entire weekend alone, dying seemed like the more appealing option. Adding to the misery were my demons, who repeatedly reminded me that I should give the kids my money now because I had no business spending it on myself. Anguish greatly surpassed rationality from day one of my depression. Like a woman who starves herself but still gains weight from a thyroid condition, I lost control over everything in my life. I often walked in circles around my apartment like a lost soul who didn't belong anywhere and had nowhere to go. Despite obsessing about suicide every day, I never considered the devastation that I was going to cause my friends and loved ones. Depression did a damn good job of preventing me from thinking about the consequences or focusing on anything but my pain. Someone once asked me, "Did you really believe no one would miss you?" The fact that I thought even my children wouldn't care shows how powerful and crippling depression can be.

Based on my loved ones' reactions upon my awakening from the coma, everyone would've blamed themselves. My mom would've pinned it on my upbringing, Alyce should've known I was depressed, Morgan was mean to me during the divorce, and Myles didn't answer my last text that said, "I love you." When people kill themselves, it seems like loved ones need a concrete reason—perhaps out of guilt or for closure. Despite scribbling a diary entry that said I couldn't deal with the upcoming holiday weekend, no one would accept that as my reason for dying. They needed something more concrete since no one kills themselves because of a silly holiday.

But yeah, they do, and I'm proof.

I've heard that most people describe their suicide attempt as going on autopilot, and that's a perfect description. Once the decision was made, I acted like a robot with my only emotions being the butterflies that filled my stomach with anticipation. The fear was gone—just like that. The best way to describe how I felt was the euphoria that a single person experiences when they realize they've finally found the one.

June 27, 2016

I'm sure that ten people would describe their suicidal tendencies in ten different ways with one exception—it's always about killing the unimaginable pain.

Now that committing suicide was becoming a reality, control made putting everything in its place a priority. Even though I was convinced that I'd be dead within twenty-four hours, being pragmatic came naturally—one of many "Sharon contradictions." Returning my work computer was crucial since my family wouldn't know where to send it. I also needed to print out a suicide note at work because someone might accidentally snatch it at a public printer and try to intervene. Worrying about odd things like the work computer and freshening up my spotless apartment were at the top of my delusional list. Even now, when people ask for the details of what happened, I hear myself telling a story that sounds like fiction.

But, at the time, it felt completely normal that I was "responsible Sharon" up until the very end. Besides itemizing my jewelry for sentimental and monetary value, the only emotional behavior I exhibited was texting both children, "I love you." As usual, Myles read my text but didn't respond—guilt would've haunted him for eternity if I'd died. Morgan immediately questioned why I texted her that message. I replied, "What are you talking about? I always say I love you." Her response was, "You only say it after a conversation." Morgan and I are very much alike, so it doesn't surprise me that her intuition went into overdrive. Fortunately, she dropped the interrogation quickly. Sending the kids one last emotional text, while not being one iota in touch with my feelings, might win the award for the biggest "Sharon contradiction" of all.

Not wanting to inconvenience anyone, even in death, I wrote a note providing Ed with all my passwords. It never occurred to me that committing suicide and turning my loved one's lives upside down was as disruptive as life gets. I envisioned the kids being upset at the funeral before quickly getting over it. Depression was protecting me from feeling because it was dead set on killing me. Now that I'm getting better every day, I realize that my demons made my feelings of worthlessness and not being loved all too real. No one could've convinced me otherwise until almost two hundred Xanax pills couldn't take me down.

Sixty-ninth Street Suicide

On Monday, June 27, I exercised early, like any other normal day. Afterward, I showered, dried my hair, packed up my computer and pushed my way onto the crowded subway. In my mind, this was my last commute, so I wanted to absorb everything that I loved so much about New York City. The first thing that I observed was the colorful mixture of passengers standing within inches of each other's faces while trying as hard as possible not to make eye contact. A homeless man was sprawled out on the entire corner seat, his stench warning everyone to stay far away. Parents were escorting their kids with colorful backpacks weighing them down to school. A young couple kissed goodbye as the man hopped off the train two stops before his girlfriend's. Commuting to and from work played a big role in my city life and was one of the things that I'd miss most. Here I was, being nostalgic about the city while I didn't give my loved ones a second thought.

After waving my office pass to Yvonne at the building's front desk, the elevator whisked me up fourteen floors to the modern office I once considered my happy place. As usual, I was the first to arrive. So, I immediately began walking from one end of the floor that always made my rubber-bottom shoes squeak to the other to turn on the lights. I continued my morning routine in the kitchen, where I brewed a steaming hot cup of Earl Gray tea. After adding my usual milk and way too much sweetener for one cup, I grabbed a cold bottle of water with my other hand on the way out. As coworkers sauntered into work an hour later in "I'm-not-a-morning-person" slow motion, I greeted them with the obligatory hello. Since I believed that no one could care less what happened to me, I didn't feel sentimental greeting them for what was supposed to be the last time.

Settling into work by ten o'clock, I completed the one writing assignment on my plate and emailed it to the account person. Now it was time to tend to the important stuff like tackling my note to Ed with all my passwords. Before printing it out, I tested the copier by sending a random document to print. When the still-warm paper sitting in the gray tray gave me the all-clear, I ran to my computer and bolted back after hitting send. Once the incriminating evidence was safely tucked in the back pocket of my jeans, I erased any trace of it. I then breathed a huge sigh of relief, knowing that my suicide mission was all systems go. By noon, I was dreading the thought of spending another five hours at work. I passed the time by eating lunch with coworkers in the kitchen. But I felt awkward knowing the huge secret that they would soon be trying to comprehend. Lunch consisted of a measly granola bar since I was keeping my stomach as empty as possible for the big event. No last meal. While feeling pain was my biggest fear, throwing up the pills was my greatest concern. At the end of the day, I checked to ensure that my computer would be easily found before pushing in the black leather chair that cramped my back despite its ergonomic design. At five o'clock on the dot, I scooted out to repeat the always fascinating subway ride home.

What saved me is the one thing that I purposely didn't do. I didn't give anyone a heads up that I'd be out of the office the following day. My thinking was that coworkers would try to get in touch with me the day after I went MIA, while I was cold and dead but not yet decomposing. This somewhat odd way of thinking is the only thing that kept me alive. I wouldn't have survived another hour, let alone another day, if I wasn't found the following morning. The idea not to call in sick struck me a few weeks earlier when no one was concerned about a missing coworker. But he routinely disappeared, so people were too busy being pissed off to worry about him. I assumed that the same would happen with me. Coworkers wouldn't realize something was amiss, or freak out, when I initially went missing. No one in the office, or in the world for that matter, gave a crap about me. So, why would they care about my well-being?

Time to Go

For more than four years, I'd drafted suicide notes to Ed, Morgan and Myles. But after rereading them at a later date, I never liked what I wrote and kept revising them. I'm not sure if it's possible to write a

Sixty-ninth Street Suicide

perfect suicide note. There are way too many things to say and no good way to express them. Right before downing the Xanax pills, I deleted the previously written notes on my computer and scribbled one last page in my journal. I ended my succinct note with "I love you" because that's the last thing I wanted Ed and the kids to ever hear from me.

Last Entry In My Journal

I am so sorry. I just cannot stand another day, especially with the long weekend looming. Most people look forward to the holidays—I dread it.

I've been alone for over ten long years. I don't want to live like this anymore. Please don't think me a coward. If it was easy, I would've done it a long time ago. I have thought about it so much and stocked up on Xanax in case I ever found the courage. My worst nightmare is dying alone. Looks like I'm facing my worst nightmare.

Ed – Morgan – Myles – I love you so much. I know you don't understand any of this, but I will be your angel and take care of you. I have so much to say but no strength to say it.

I'm sorry. I love you all.

In addition, I pulled out a piece of crisp pink stationery to compose an apology note for whoever was inconvenienced by finding me—I was considerate to the end. I placed the Living Will I'd drawn up in 2012—for just this moment—on the end table. It was supposed to ensure that no one would keep me alive by extraordinary measures. At the time, I was unaware that Do Not Resuscitate doesn't apply outside the hospital. That meant the paramedics were obligated to provide medical care when they found me in my apartment. If they hadn't immediately intubated me, the odds are that I would've died on the way from my apartment on Sixty-Ninth Street to the hospital a mere two blocks away.

Everything seemed to be in order by seven o'clock on what I was expecting to be my last day alive. I felt no fear—motivation had taken its place. Ready to go, I excitedly grabbed all four bottles of Xanax out of my private hoarding cabinet. I then nearly skipped to the kitchen before lining them up on the counter like little toy soldiers—my favorite bottle with a combined three-month supply was placed in the back for last. I then took a bottle of apple sauce out of the fridge because I'd read that it coats the stomach and helps prevent vomiting during an overdose. The only reason that I didn't add Oxycodone to the mix was that I was afraid of throwing up—which happened once after popping just one pill following an ankle surgery. Later on, I was told that mixing two hundred Xanax pills with Oxycodone would've undoubtedly made my so-called serious suicide a successful suicide. Before undressing, I placed an oversized industrial black plastic bag under the bed. I didn't want to inconvenience my downstairs neighbors with my decomposing fluids dripping from their ceiling.

Upon feeling satisfied that everything was in its place, I hung up that day's clothing, stepped into my pajamas and headed toward the bathroom. There, I combed my hair, removed my makeup, moisturized my skin and brushed my teeth. I don't recall feeling sad or nostalgic while looking in the mirror for what was supposed to be the last time. Detaching made my final minutes on earth emotionally pain-free. It felt like my demons were leading the way, and I was simply following their motions. After a few minutes, I finished the nighttime routine that I'd followed for years, with the exception of putting in my night guard. Clenching my teeth was now the least of my worries. I was now ready to gulp down the pills, fall asleep and end the pain by killing myself. When I walked back to my typically small NYC kitchen, I opened one bottle of Xanax at a time and put it straight to my lips. I gulped down all the pills at once by tilting my head back like I did as a child when I was eating a bunch of chiclets. After each bottle, I drank water and swallowed a spoonful or two of apple sauce before waiting a minute to let the pills settle. When I was done, I placed the bottles back in a row on the counter to show whoever found me what I'd swallowed. I then oddly popped a few Advil PM to help me sleep—as if taking almost two hundred Xanax pills wasn't enough. I considered swallowing my blood thinner, but I was trying to avoid pain at all costs and bleeding out like an Ebola victim didn't seem particularly pleasant.

Now that I was ready to die, my last act was looking up toward the ceiling and apologizing to all the friends and relatives who I'd soon be reuniting with in heaven. Not for a second did I consider the loved ones on earth I was about to leave behind, including my two beautiful children. Subconsciously shutting out my love for them was probably the only way that I could leave them without a mother. Like any other night, I quickly fell asleep on my stomach. My soft, plush red blanket was pulled tightly up to my neck, despite it being a warm summer's evening. The plan was to go from sleep to unconsciousness to death. This was not a cry for help. I didn't want to be saved, and the possibility of survival was never a part of the equation.

Yet, the next thing I remember is slowly waking up six days later.

Somehow, I'd survived.

I'm not sure if I live happily ever after, but I do know that I live. And for now, that's enough.

Epilogue

I wish I'd recognized my depression so that I could've gotten better without having to almost die and put my family through hell. But for me, reaching below rock bottom was what I needed to finally understand that there was a way out. I wasn't a failure, I wasn't hopeless, and I wasn't alone.

Now that I've put my experience into context, I'm intent on sharing it with the world. Those who are suffering from depression need to know that they're not alone. Families need to understand how mental illness distorts a sufferer's reality. Friends and family might not visibly see the pain, but it's real and all-encompassing. Until the stigma of mental illness, and particularly suicide, is eradicated, people will suffer—and often die—alone.

Don't wait, get help.

There are people who love you!!!

The National Suicide Prevention Lifeline is a United States-based suicide prevention network of over 160 crisis centers that provides 24/7 service via a toll-free hotline: 1-800-273-8255. It is available to anyone in suicidal crisis or emotional distress.

Acknowledgements

To my beautiful children Morgan and Myles, my mom, Alyce, Lolly pup and my father in heaven—who is the only reason I'm alive today. To love so deeply, I have no words.

To depression, I raise both middle fingers and salute you.

About the Author

Sharon was born a writer and currently puts food on the table as a financial content writer. She was inspired to share her lifelong struggle with depression and suicidal thoughts after surviving a serious overdose. Sharon recently left the concrete jungle to live in sunny Florida with her quirky dachshund, Lolly. She's still getting used to having more bad hair days than good ones. When she's not immersed in her writing, you can find her intensely focusing on her newfound pastime—Mahjong.

www.ingramcontent.com/pod-product-compliance
Lightning Source LLC
Chambersburg PA
CBHW031955080426
42735CB00007B/397